FREDERICK R. WEISMAN ART FOUNDATION

Selected works from the FREDERICK R. WEISMAN ART FOUNDATION

Catalogue Editor
Nora Halpern Brougher

Catalogue Design
Lorraine Wild/Agenda

Design Assistant
Sean Adams

Research Assistants
Lisa Fredriksen
Anna Wohl

Photography
Grey Crawford
Tom Vinetz

Additional Photography
Daniel Weinberg Gallery (R. Artschwager, *Chair and Window*);
Douglas Parker (J. Goode, *Untitled*);
Stephen Callis (cover)

Typesetting
Mondo Typo, Inc., Santa Monica, CA

Color Separations
Alan Lithograph Inc., Inglewood, CA
The Castle Press, Pasadena, CA

Printing
Alan Lithograph Inc., Inglewood, CA

Special thanks
Archives of American Art, Smithsonian Institution
Deborah Briskin
Eddie Fumasi
Dave Gillespie

ISBN 0-9614537-2-9

Library of Congress Catalogue Number 88-083685

©1989 Frederick R. Weisman Art Foundation
10350 Santa Monica Boulevard, #160
Los Angeles, CA 90025

FREDERICK R. WEISMAN ART FOUNDATION

CONTENTS

The Frederick R. Weisman Art Foundation is a collection which features objects by a wide range of contemporary masters, but which emphasizes American art from the 1960s through the 1980s. Funding has been made available to continue to acquire art for the Foundation Collection, as well as to establish a program of exhibitions, symposiums and workshops which deal with issues of importance to those interested in the world of contemporary art.

The Foundation Collection, now consisting of over three hundred works, is comprised of paintings, sculptures, prints and photographs by emerging artists from around the world juxtaposed with excellent recent examples by artists whose reputations are already well established. Mr. Weisman's desire in developing such a collection was to expose and inform wide audiences on a continuing basis to international contemporary art.

With these goals in mind, the art foundation began by circulating its cross section of recent works to parts of the nation where public access to original contemporary art was limited. The first exhibition tour began at the Palm Springs Desert Museum and traveled to seven venues as diverse as the Honolulu Academy of Arts in Hawaii and the Anchorage Historical and Fine Arts Museum in Alaska.

The success of these initial exhibitions and the expansion of the collection to include increasing numbers of European and Asian artists, led to the development of an international touring program. In 1985, the Foundation Collection was divided into two segments, each consisting of about one hundred works which visited eleven museums in France, Israel, Hong Kong, Japan, Korea, Portugal and Switzerland.

The most recent traveling exhibition program consisted of tours to six American museums during 1987 and 1988. Beginning at The Baltimore Museum of Art, the show traveled to the Pennsylvania Academy of the Fine Arts, Birmingham Museum of Art, Norton Gallery and School of Art in West Palm Beach, Florida, the Colorado Springs Fine Arts Center and New Orleans Museum of Art.

For 1989 and 1990, the Foundation is again circulating two exhibitions. This, the primary grouping, has been curated by Edith Tonelli, Director and Elizabeth Shepherd, Curator of the Wight Art Gallery at UCLA and Nora Halpern Brougher. After the opening at UCLA, the exhibition will travel to three additional venues. The second, somewhat smaller exhibition recently opened in El Paso, TX/Las Cruces, NM and will travel to four other institutions across the country.

These presentations, which have proven to be a popular centerpiece for the Frederick R. Weisman Art Foundation activities, have fulfilled this purpose of offering a diverse and inquisitive public a fresh perspective on current directions in art. It is Mr. Weisman's belief, and ours, that art has a powerful capacity to help us communicate and that exhibitions such as these can enhance our understanding of one another.

Henry T. Hopkins

Director, Frederick R. Weisman
Art Foundation

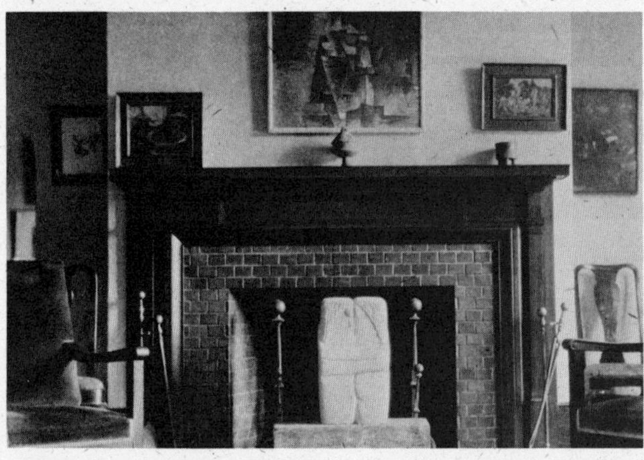

Interior, Walter and Louise Arensberg home
(circa 1942).
Photo: Beatrice Wood.

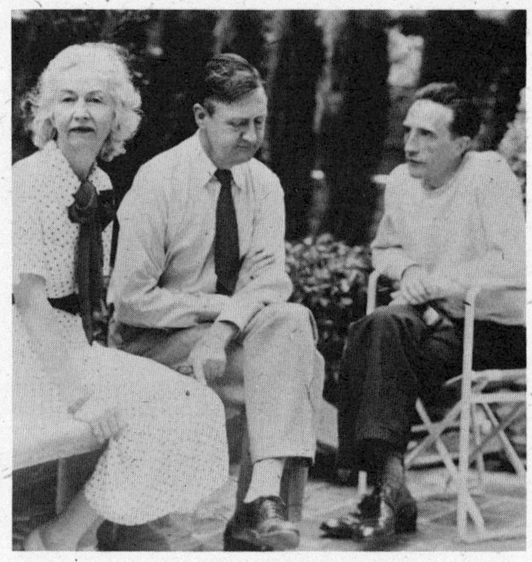

The Arensbergs with Marcel Duchamp
(circa 1942).
Photo: Beatrice Wood.

In 1918, when the young Frederick Weisman moved here with his family from Minneapolis, Los Angeles was known mainly as an agricultural area with potential for oil development. It had also recently begun to absorb an influx of East Coast theatrical types who gravitated toward the new film studios in and around Hollywood. As it began to grow creatively and industrially, Los Angeles entered a period of rapid cultural maturation. For most of the first two decades of the twentieth-century, San Francisco had been California's premier metropolis, the state's first "real" city; with its eyes to the East, it had grown into a hilly hybrid of Boston and Philadelphia. Los Angeles was seen as a younger, underdeveloped sibling, a renegade that came to resemble less its Eastern parents than neighboring Mexico and the "wilder" West. Capitalizing on its newness, Los Angeles, like an oversized adolescent, developed into a gawky conglomeration of non-neighborhoods. One of this country's true urban frontiers, the growing city encouraged — and continues to encourage — the sprawl of individual communities. Early in this century, it began to attract and cultivate many visionaries who made far-reaching contributions in business and the arts. It was in this unique environment of wide-open horizons and seemingly endless innovation that Frederick Weisman was raised.

A year after the Weisman's arrival, the population of Los Angeles topped that of San Francisco, making it California's largest city. In 1921 Walter and Louise Arensberg moved to Los Angeles from New York. Over the next several decades, they were to become the city's leading patrons of contemporary art. The Arensbergs' extensive collection, ultimately donated to the Philadelphia Museum of Art, had the most comprehensive concentration in the world of works by Marcel Duchamp as well as pieces by Wassily Kandinsky, Paul Klee, Francis Picabia, Pablo Picasso, and Man Ray, among others. The Arensberg home was a meeting place for artists, collectors, and intellectuals. Together with art supporters such as Vincent Price, Edward G. Robinson, Galka Scheyer, and Jake Zeitlin, the Arensbergs helped to give Los Angeles its start as a contemporary art center by providing exposure for burgeoning artists.

The city's cultural environment was further enhanced by the presence of many of the period's most avant-garde figures. Duchamp, Max Ernst, Man Ray, and Dorothea Tanning spent a great deal of time in Los Angeles in the 1920s, '30s and '40s. Fernand Léger taught at Claremont College (just east of Los Angeles) in 1930, and in 1931 Hans Hoffman held classes at the Chouinard Art Institute in the downtown area.

The rise of Nazism in Europe drove a large number of artists and intellectuals to freedom in the United States; the temperate climate and cultural attractions of Southern California drew many people there. Writers such as Thomas Mann and Bertolt Brecht came for long stays, and musical pioneers such as Arnold Schoenberg and Gregor Piatagorsky settled permanently.

Although the gallery scene did not prove to be commercially viable in this period, Los Angeles gallery-goers were nevertheless able to see works by many local artists as well as by Alexei Jawlensky, Kandinsky, Klee, Léger, and Henri Matisse. In the late '30s, Picasso's *Guernica* was on view at Stendahl's Wilshire Boulevard gallery space. By the 1940s, local galleries were showing works by Surrealists such as Ernst, René Magritte, and Yves Tanguy. The presence of these various artists and their works did much to solidify the city's cultural base and build support for contemporary art. It also no doubt influenced the growth of young artists such as Philip Guston and Jackson Pollock, both of whom grew up and studied in Los Angeles.

Frederick Weisman came of age in the flourishing city at about the same time as Guston and Pollock. Although he did not become actively involved in the Los Angeles art world as a young man, he was aware of and avidly interested in the visual arts. He frequented local galleries and the Los Angeles County Museum, then housed downtown in Exposition Park. Weisman began to collect at an early age, gathering an array

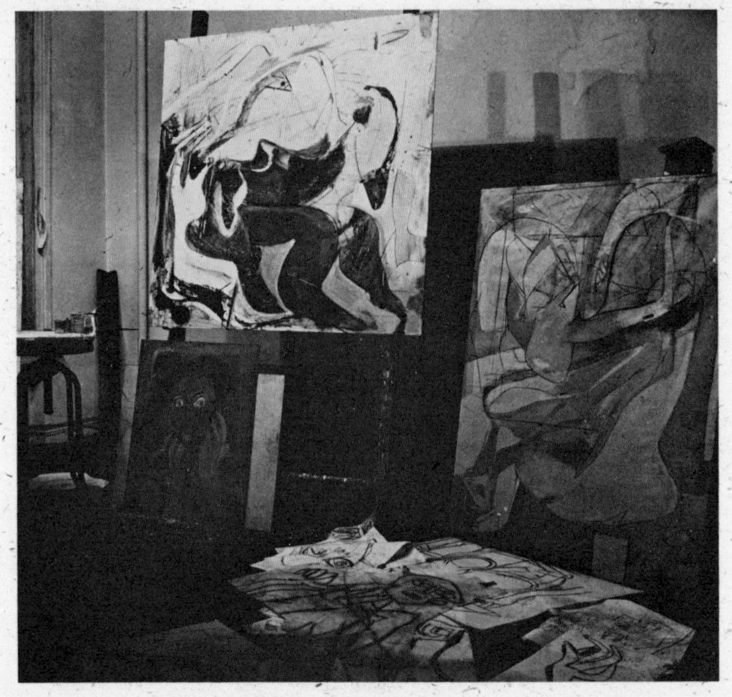

Willem de Kooning's studio
(circa 1946).
Lower right, the artist's *Pink Angels* (circa 1945, oil on canvas),
now in Frederick Weisman's collection.
Photo: Harry Bowden Papers, Archives of American Art,
Smithsonian Institution.

of art posters and prints as well as an extensive grouping of nineteenth- and early twentieth-century stamps and coins.

Weisman begin acquiring art on a modest scale in the late 1940s, not making what he considered to be major purchases until he acquired a Jean Arp bronze and a Jawlensky oil on canvas in the late '50s. He was greatly influenced by the New York collector-turned-dealer Ben Heller, who introduced him to the art of the American Abstract Expressionist movement. Before meeting Heller, Weisman had concentrated his attention on European art of the pre- and post-World War II eras, collecting works by abstractionists such as Pierre Soulages and Lucio Fontana. Upon seeing his first Franz Kline, however, he became involved almost exclusively with the work of American artists. Artworks by Kline as well as by Arshile Gorky, Willem de Kooning, Barnett Newman, Pollock, and Mark Rothko quickly became part of his collection. Weisman developed a close relationship with Clyfford Still and early on in the artist's career, he bought two large canvases, the first of a number he would collect. In 1963, Still sent him a large yellow untitled work from 1951 as a "declaration of independence" gift, acknowledging that his support had enabled him to move out of New York and into a studio in Westminster, Maryland.

Weisman encouraged many other artists at early points in their careers. Works by Morris Louis, Kenneth Noland, Ad Reinhardt, and, later, Jasper Johns, Roy Lichtenstein, Robert Rauschenberg, and Andy Warhol came to hang on the walls of his Beverly Hills home. Pieces by California artists Larry Bell, Billy Al Bengston, Bruce Conner, Sam Francis, Robert Graham, Robert Irwin, Edward Kienholz, and Edward Ruscha were hung prominently in Weisman's home. Sculptures by artists such as John McCracken, Kenneth Price, and Peter Voulkos were also included in his collection.

Like the Arensbergs before him, Weisman opened his home to many artists and historians. Clement Greenberg, Harold Rosenberg, William Seitz, and other leading theoreticians gave talks to local collectors, curators and artists using the Weisman home as a forum for the exchange of ideas. Weisman also worked with other local collectors to establish the Modern and Contemporary Art Council, a support group for the Los Angeles County Museum of Art's twentieth-century department created in 1962. Still active today, the council promotes interest and involvement in contemporary art through lectures and discussions and through its joint sponsorship with the museum of the annual Young Talent Award, established in 1963 to recognize significant emerging artists.

As a trustee of the Los Angeles County Museum of Art and the Pasadena Art Museum, Weisman played a vital role in helping to shape the highly creative staffs of those institutions. Curators such as James Demetrion, James Elliott, Barbara Haskell, Henry Hopkins, Walter Hopps, and Jane Livingston all worked locally in the mid- to late '60s. At the same time, *Artforum* magazine, under the tutelage of Philip Leider and John Coplans, became an important voice for contemporary art criticism and theory. As in the flourishing period of the 1920s and '30s, Los Angeles was again an intellectual center for the arts.

Although the city continued to grow in the late 1960s and early '70s, the local art scene settled down and seemed to take a breather. Many of the intellectuals who had been driving forces in the area moved to other cities. In 1967 *Artforum* transplanted itself to New York, and in 1973 Southern California lost one of its few institutional champions of contemporary art when the Pasadena Art Museum closed its doors.

In 1982, Mr. Weisman established the Frederick R. Weisman Art Foundation, whose collection is characterized by a scope and purpose that distinguish it from the other two collections he developed previously. The first of these was the personal collection. The second, focusing mainly on Japanese contemporary art, was assembled primarily to enhance the working environment of Mr. Weisman's corporate headquarters in Glen Burnie, Maryland. The Foundation Collection, which for a period was known as the Frederick R. Weisman

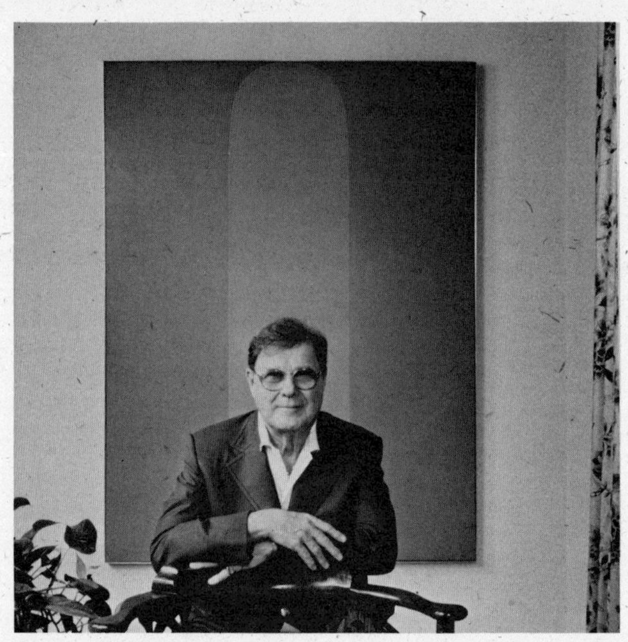

Frederick Weisman in his Los Angeles home (1986).
Behind, Ellsworth Kelly's *Red-Orange Blue* (1964–1965,
oil on canvas). Photo: Arnold Newman.

Collection, was organized with the primary purpose of broadening public knowledge about developments in contemporary art through an extensive touring program. Spanning the period from 1946 to the present, the Foundation Collection contains more than three hundred works, including examples by many of the same artists whose works are displayed in Mr. Weisman's home. The collection also features works by younger and emerging artists, providing many of them with their first exposure to a wide audience. Mr. Weisman's aim in creating such a collection has been to reach an audience on a continuing basis and thus help to inspire an ongoing examination of international developments in contemporary art.

With these goals in mind, the Foundation Collection began to circulate its cross section of recent works to parts of the nation where public access to original works of contemporary art was limited. The first exhibition was at the Palm Springs Desert Museum, followed by showings at the Albuquerque Museum; Honolulu Academy of Arts; San Francisco Art Institute Galleries; Utah Museum of Fine Arts, Salt Lake City; Nora Eccles Harrison Museum, Logan, Utah; Anchorage Historical and Fine Arts Museum; University of Arizona Museum of Art, Tucson; and Art Center College of Design, Pasadena. The success of these initial exhibitions and the expansion of the Foundation Collection to include increasing numbers of European and Asian artists led to the development of an international touring program. In 1985 the foundation collection was divided into two segments, each consisting of about one hundred works, which visited eleven museums in France, Israel, Hong Kong, Japan, Korea, Portugal, and Switzerland. In 1987 and 1988 an exhibition of sixty-five works toured the United States, making stops at The Baltimore Museum of Art; Pennsylvania Academy of the Fine Arts; Birmingham Museum of Art; Norton Gallery and School of Art, West Palm Beach; Colorado Springs Fine Arts Center; New Orleans Museum of Art; Walker Art Center; and San Antonio Art Institute. Together, the national and international tours have exposed tens of thousands of people to an array of vigorous new art and to familiar works that they may have seen before only in reproduction. The exhibitions have proven especially valuable to art students, enhancing their first-hand knowledge of current work.

The Frederick R. Weisman Art Foundation looks forward to continuing its support of current developments in art on an international level. It is the Foundation's hope to remain involved in the discovery of new work and to continue to expand public awareness and appreciation of the rich history of contemporary art.

Nora Halpern Brougher

Curator, Frederick R. Weisman
Art Foundation

All my activities in art and business are an attempt to bring the world closer together. The language of art is universal. I don't think there's anything that communicates better than art. I realize that's a big statement, but art's quicker than language and clearer than philosophy.

Frederick R. Weisman

Frederick R. Weisman, who lives in Los Angeles and operates out of corporate headquarters between Baltimore and Washington, D.C., is a cheerful, modest, approachable man, who belies the stereotypical image of a tycoon. President at the age of thirty-one of Hunt Foods, Inc., with which he was affiliated for eighteen years, Weisman retired from the food industry in 1958. Today the Frederick Weisman Company, which employs five hundred people and has eight subsidiaries, is among the largest revenue producers in Maryland. Diversified interests include computers, real estate, insurance, and Mid-Atlantic Toyota Distributors, Inc., acquired in 1970 and now one of the leading distributors of Toyota cars and trucks in the United States.

Weisman's corporate collection consists almost entirely of Japanese art since the Edo period; its primary focus is twentieth-century paintings, sculptures, ceramics, and prints. Weisman began collecting Japanese art in 1972 just prior to moving his Toyota company to new headquarters in Glen Burnie, Maryland. Designed by Frank Gehry, the headquarters building features pastel walls and chain-link room dividers. Oriental art provides a fine contrast to the rough and ready structure. "The design of the facility was very controversial," Weisman recalls. "When it first opened, someone commented, 'This is a beautiful building, but when do they put on the roof?' The building's only formal space is a traditional tearoom constructed by Japanese craftsmen, and we use it to entertain visiting businessmen in a style to which they are accustomed to at home. Our corporate facilities are open for public tours, and we encourage schools in surrounding communities to bring over their students."

Gehry's fresh architectural ideas helped to stimulate an ingenious approach to collecting art by emerging talents. About fifteen years ago, for example, when Weisman was in Kyoto, Japan he was struck by the work of a young artist named Ueda and purchased a large sculpture reminiscent of an automobile – two enormous bronze wheels connected by colored rope – for the reception area of the Glen Burnie building. On a visit to Kyoto last September, Weisman saw a retrospective of Ueda's work and was gratified to discover that an artist whose work he had acquired long ago was the subject of a museum exhibition.

Weisman refuses on principal to keep works in storage, for he believes that when he buys work by a living artist he has a responsibility to display it. The Frederick R. Weisman Art Foundation collection includes paintings by Abstract Expressionist artists such as Arshile Gorky and Barnett Newman, which function as historical reference points, as well as Pop, Minimalist, Conceptual, and Neo-Expressionist works of seminal importance. "I love observing exhibition goers in places like Seoul or Yokohama," commented Weisman. "They're thrilled by the opportunity to see original works and meet artists like Jasper Johns, Ellsworth Kelly, and Alex Katz, names they previously knew only through poster reproductions and books."

When Foundation exhibitions are installed, paintings and sculptures by emerging artists are placed adjacent to more famous works. By putting younger artists in the context of older, more renowned talents, the quality of their work, which has nothing to do with age or reputation, is underscored. According to Weisman, "A fine work of art is a fine work of art. By supporting emerging artists I try to demonstrate that you don't have to have lots of money to form a distinctive collection."

Weisman has not yet identified a permanent home for the Foundation, although he has concluded that no already-established entity is large enough to exhibit his entire holdings. In addition, the concept of donating to a museum that would not place the work on continuous view or might eventually deacquisition objects, is a disagreeable prospect. To bring leadership to his programs, Weisman appointed Henry T. Hopkins, former director of the San Francisco Museum of Modern Art, as Foundation director in November 1986. Hopkins commands the foundation's annual acquisitions budget and has begun, with curator Nora Halpern Brougher, to refine eclectic and scattered aspects of the collection into a coherent whole. According to Hopkins, "A collection built on an individual collector's intuition offers a lively alternative to the market-dominated collecting patterns of larger museums, which are becoming standardized."

The Foundation is collaborating with universities, providing opportunities for graduate students to research the collection and prepare exhibitions. Programs have been initiated at the University of Maryland, and at Colgate and Tulane Universities. Gifts of significant works by contemporary artists have been made to many cultural institutions in the United States, including most centers visited by the Foundation's traveling exhibitions. The Foundation has also stepped up its program of lending American art abroad, with works presently on view at American embassies in Japan, Korea, and Russia; it also has lent work by California artists to Senators Alan Cranston and Pete Wilson for their Washington, D.C. offices as well as placed work on public view in Los Angeles' City Hall.

In January 1989, the first in a continuing series of workshops will be held under the Foundation's auspices, to consider the integration of art and architecture. An international roster of artists, architects, and scholars will participate in a private, unstructured roundtable discussion. The Foundation hopes that several days of informal, focused discourse will result in a ground-breaking publication. Among the other ambitious new program initiatives is the fostering of exchanges of art exhibitions and artists between Los Angeles and its sister cities; Berlin, Vancouver, Nagoya, Mexico City, Bordeaux and Athens. 1989 will also mark the establishment of the Frederick R. Weisman Art Foundation Award for creativity in the arts. Awards will be given to both established and to unknown artists recommended by a panel of expert advisers.

Mr. Weisman's personal collection, which he foresees will eventually become part of the Foundation, can't easily be pigeonholed. Housed in his sprawling Spanish Colonial mansion in Los Angeles, it includes works by masters such as Cézanne, Picasso, and Rothko as well as recent sensations like Keith Haring and Anselm Kiefer. Primarily devoted to art since the 1940s, the collection emphasizes American art of the '50s and '60s. There are wonderful exceptions, however, such as *Hohe Gruppe*, a 1931 painting by Paul Klee, and an imposing pastel by Picasso, *Maternité*, dating from 1921, the latter the subject of a typical Weisman anecdote. On one of his frequent trips to Japan, he met with Toshio Hara, an important contemporary art collector, who insisted that Weisman visit an associate's collection consisting mostly of works by Impressionist and Post-Impressionist artists. While conversing with Hara's associate, Weisman noticed a small reproduction of Picasso's *Maternité* and asked why this postcard was on display. "Oh, Mr. Weisman, I did a terrible thing," the associate said. "I had that and I sold it. I really shouldn't have sold it. I really feel very badly about it." Weisman replied, "If I did a terrible thing like what you're saying and I felt badly about it, I would like to know where the artwork was and if it was in a good place. I just want you to know that that Picasso is in my home in California." When Weisman returned to Los Angeles he had himself photographed in front of the painting and sent a print to the Japanese collector along with an invitation to visit anytime.

Unlike many collectors, Weisman has not been afraid to commission works of art. Recently, while visiting an artist's foundry in Birmingham, Alabama, he fell in love with the work of Frank Fleming and commissioned the artist to make a surreal bronze mailbox cupped in a large human hand that sits on a columnar forearm covered with frogs and fish. Weisman also has commissioned fountains by Vasa and Robert Graham, a stained-glass work by Matt Mullican, a gateway by DeWain Valentine, and a sculpture of his father by Duane Hanson. "You've got to be careful not to tell an artist what to do," he warns. "You can make strong suggestions, tell him your feelings, and then you need to get out of the way and let him do his work."

Weisman opens his home by invitation to groups of art lovers from all parts of the world. In this way he is fulfilling his dream of turning his house into a living museum, preserving his creative spirit and anti-art-historical bias. His personal choices, more instinctive and emotional than cerebral, do not conform to any aesthetic criterion. "I regret not buying works by Richard Diebenkorn when I first saw them," Weisman confesses. "I very much believe that he who hesitates is lost."

Wherever Weisman travels he visits museums, galleries, artists' studios, and collectors and buys what appeals to him on a gut level, making no attempt to acquire a cohesive history of any style or theme. "I try not to be impulsive," he claims. "I try to wait a little bit, to sleep on it. But I don't hesitate when something really strikes me. I just don't do things by the book. I don't ask a lawyer or a banker to make my business judgments and I don't have advisers in art. From the beginning, I've followed my feelings."

Donna Stein

*Based on interviews conducted on
May 8, 1986 and
October 10, 1988*

THE PLATES

Richard Artschwager (USA)

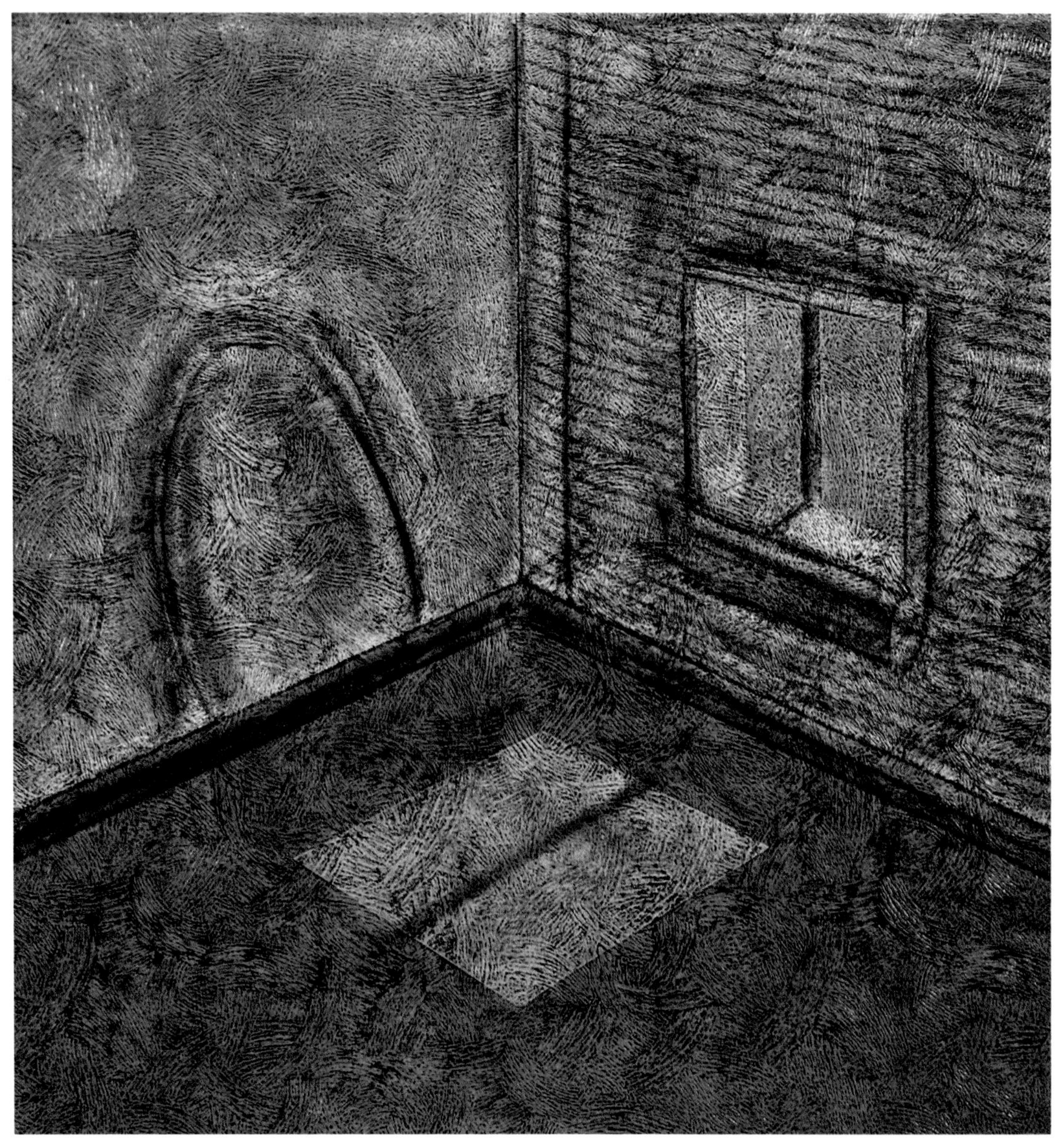

Horizontal Men, *1984*
gelatin silver prints on board
97¼ x 48⅝ in.

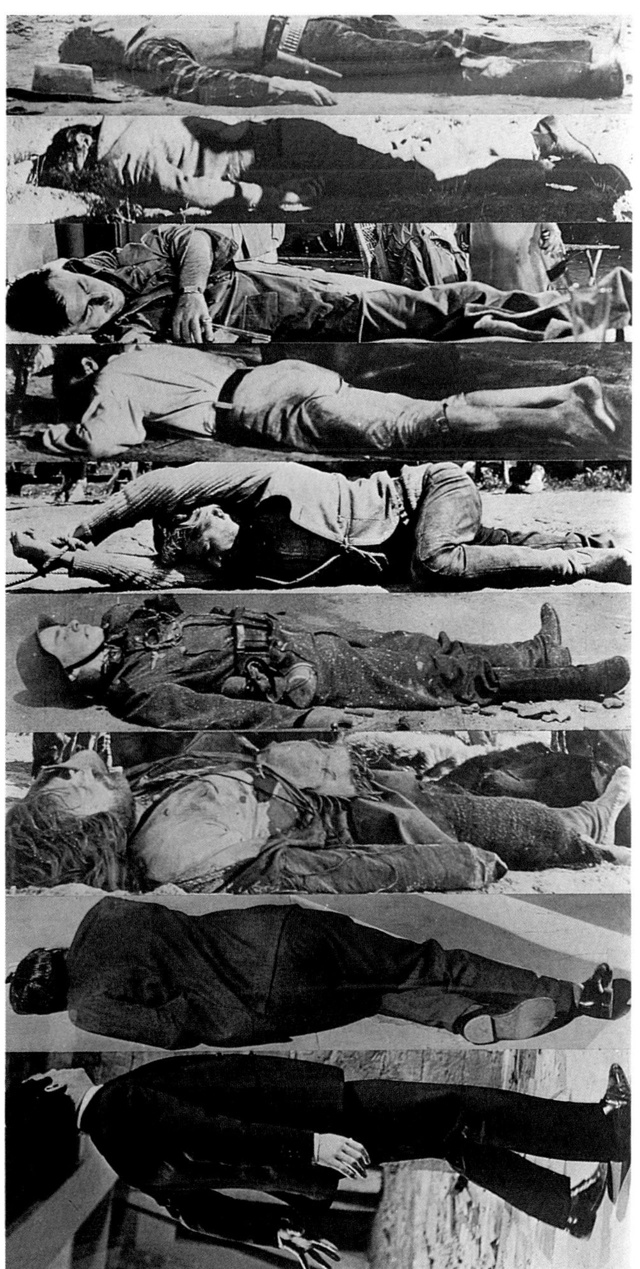

John Baldessari *(USA)*

David Bates *(USA)*

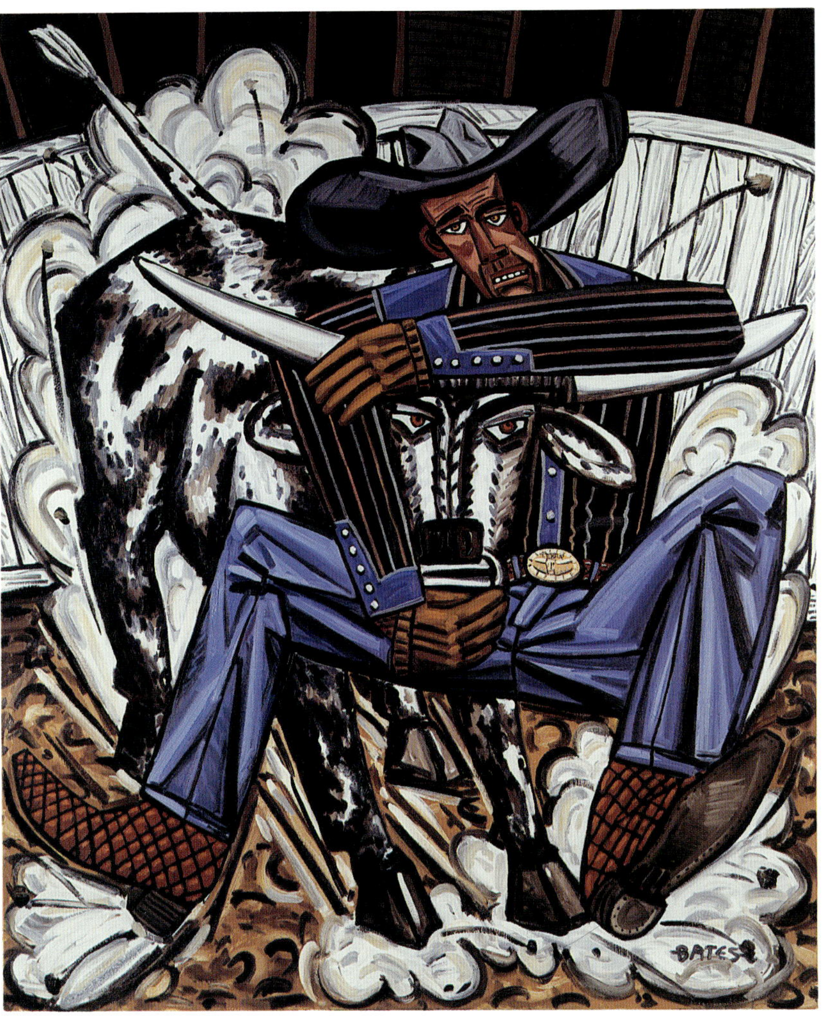

Flying Frog with Chattering Man at 2,845,322, 1983
programmed light: aluminum and thirty twelve-inch-diameter neon tubes
24 x 348 x 54 in.
man: aluminum, wood, electric motor, and speaker
82½ x 23 x 13 in.

Jonathan Borofsky *(USA)*

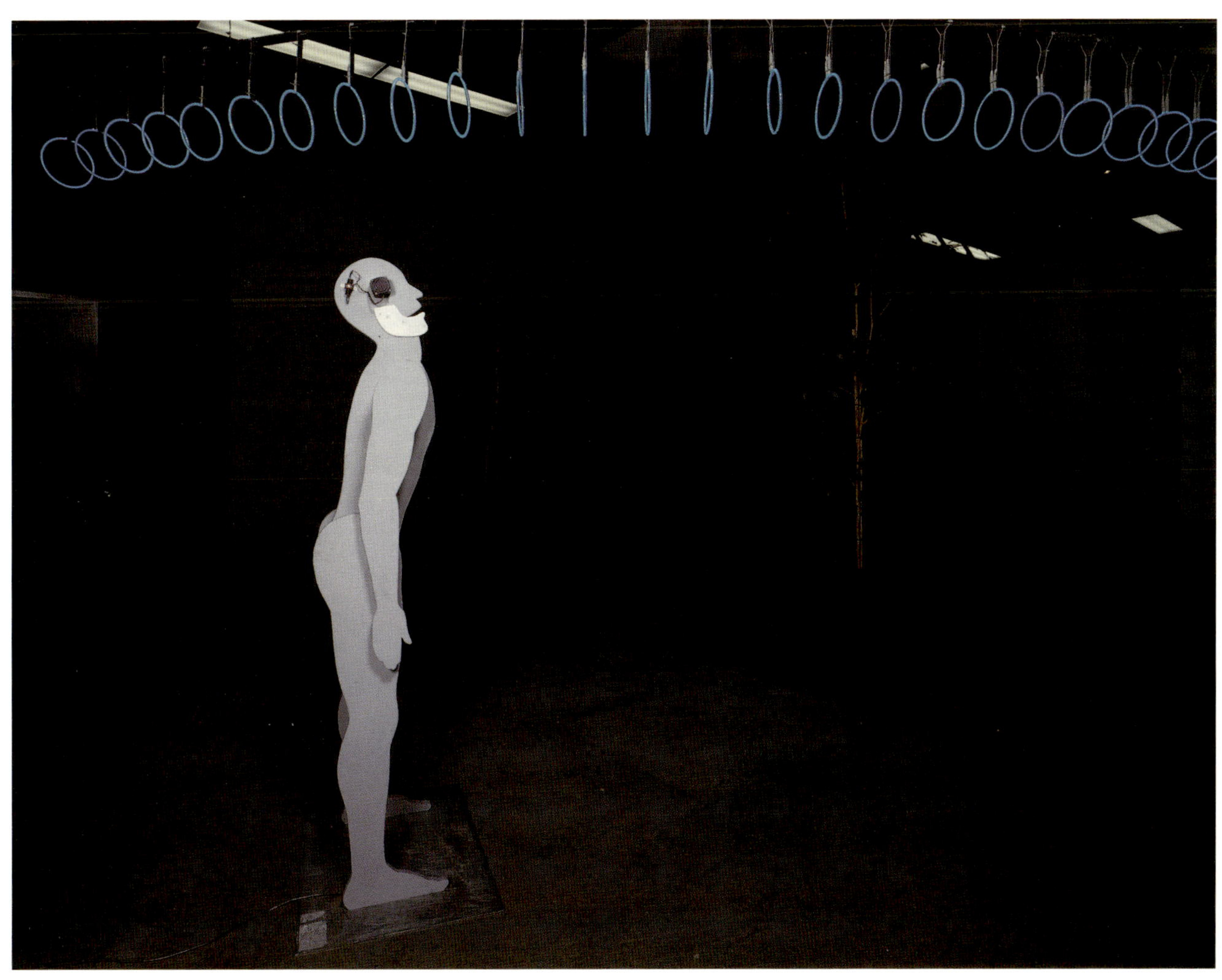

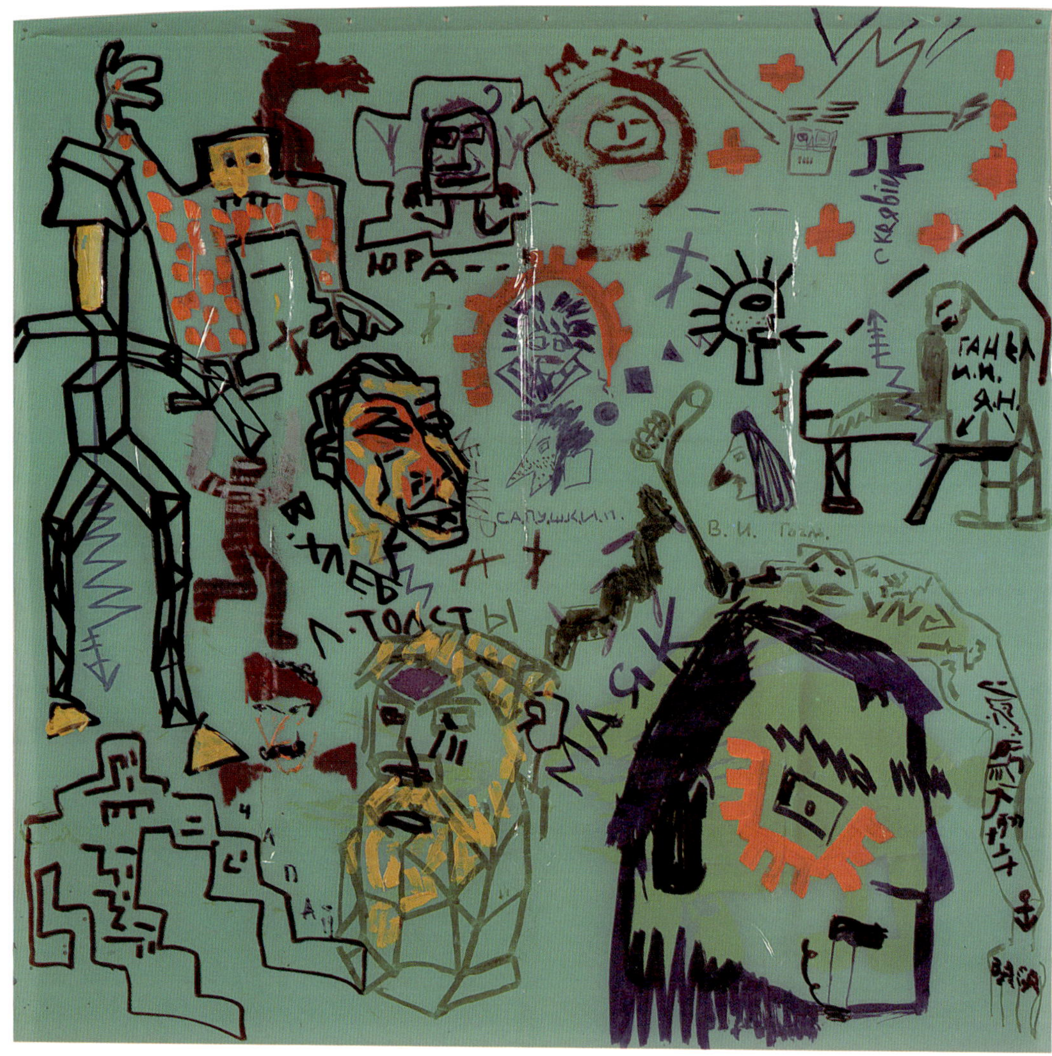

Afrika Bugaev, Oleg Kotelnikov, Andrei Krisanov, Timur Novikov, and Inal Savtchenikov *(USSR)*

Figures, 1983
Cibachrome prints with lacquer frames, ed 2/3 (diptych)
40¼ x 61¾ in. (each)

Sarah Charlesworth *(USA)*

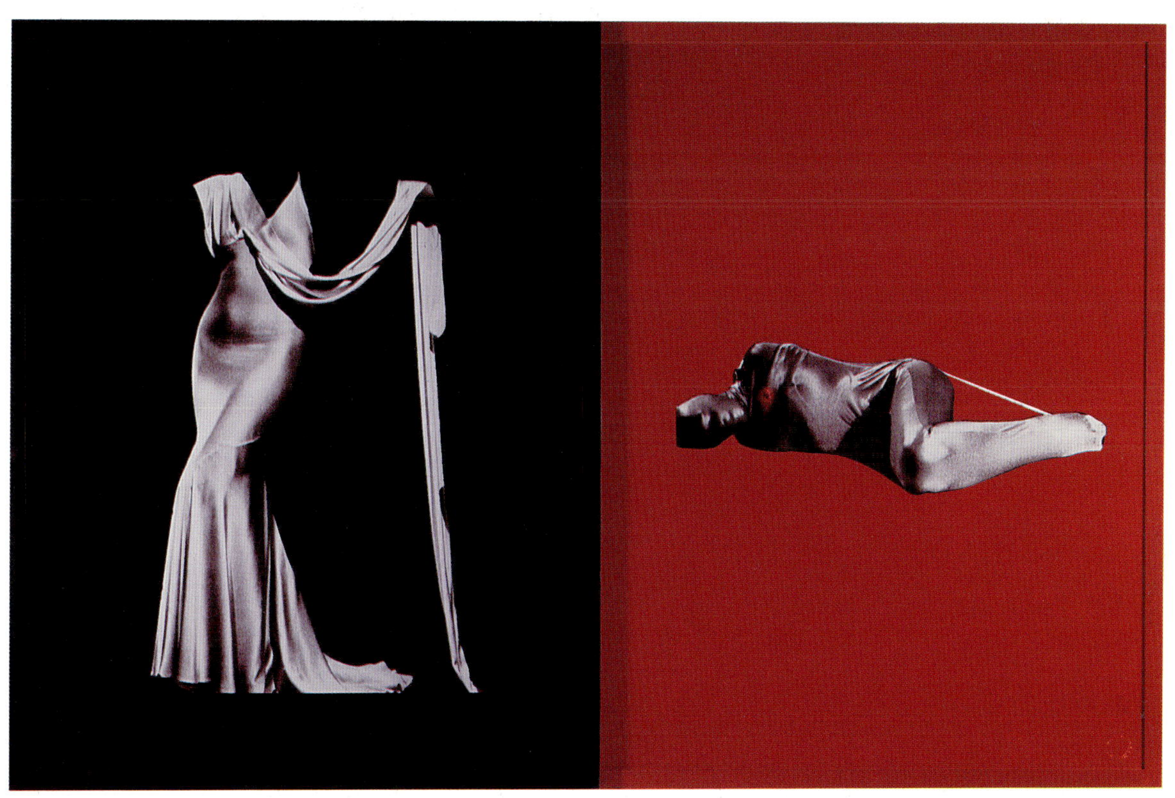

Surrounded Islands (Project for Biscayne Bay, Greater Miami,
Florida), 1982
*pastel, charcoal, pencil, crayon, fabric sample,
and photograph (two drawings)
15 x 96 in.; 42 x 96 in.*

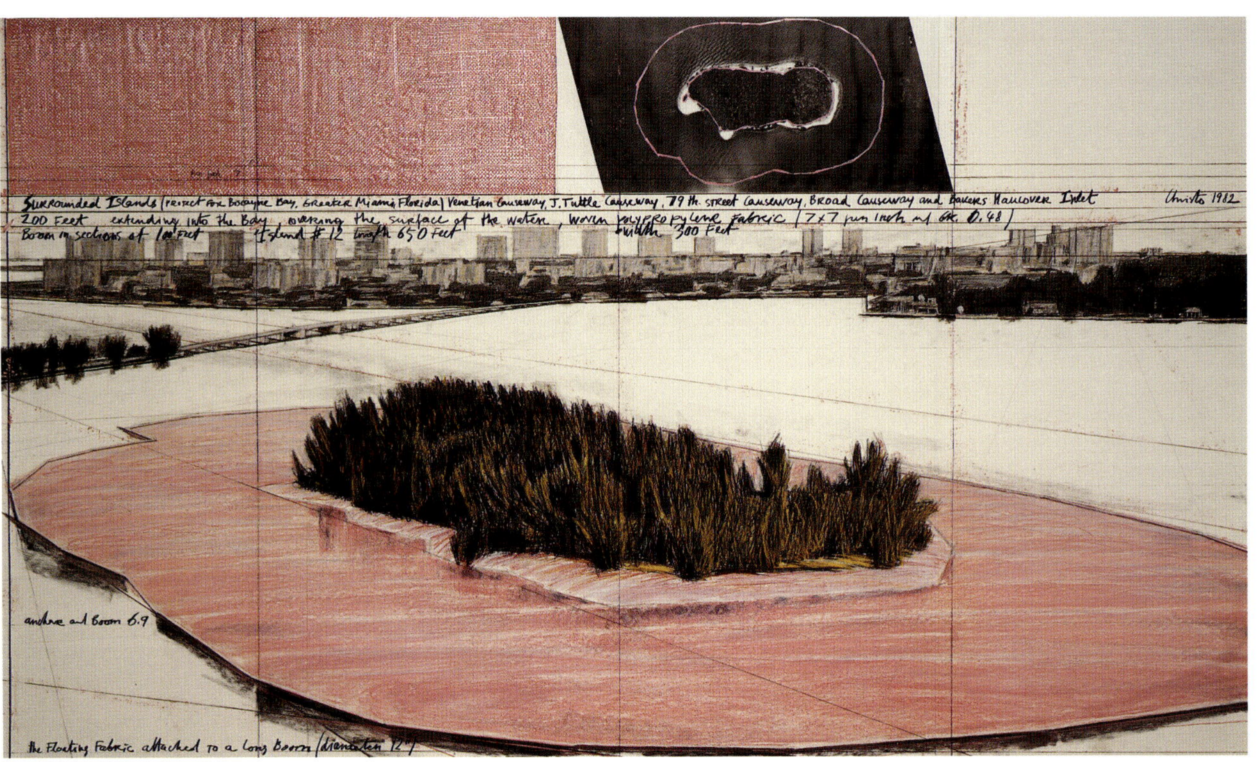

Christo (Christo Javacheff) *(Bulgaria/USA)*

Suitcase, 1962
mixed media sculpture
23 x 24 x 9 in.

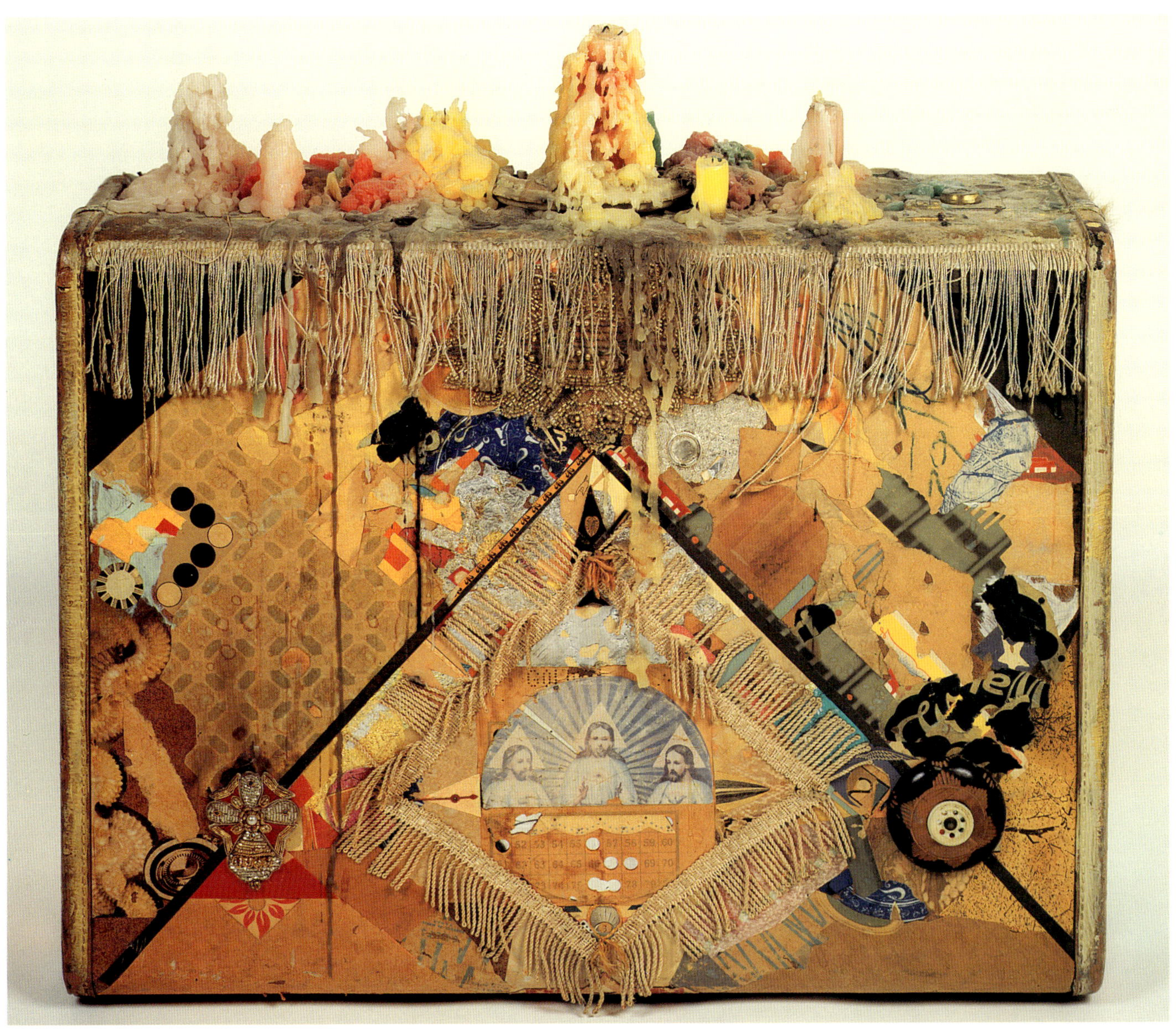

Hotel de l'Etoile, *n.d. (circa 1950–1954)*
construction with wood, paper collage, bangle, rod, wire mesh,
tempera and glass
16½ x 10½ x 4 in.

Joseph Cornell *(USA)*

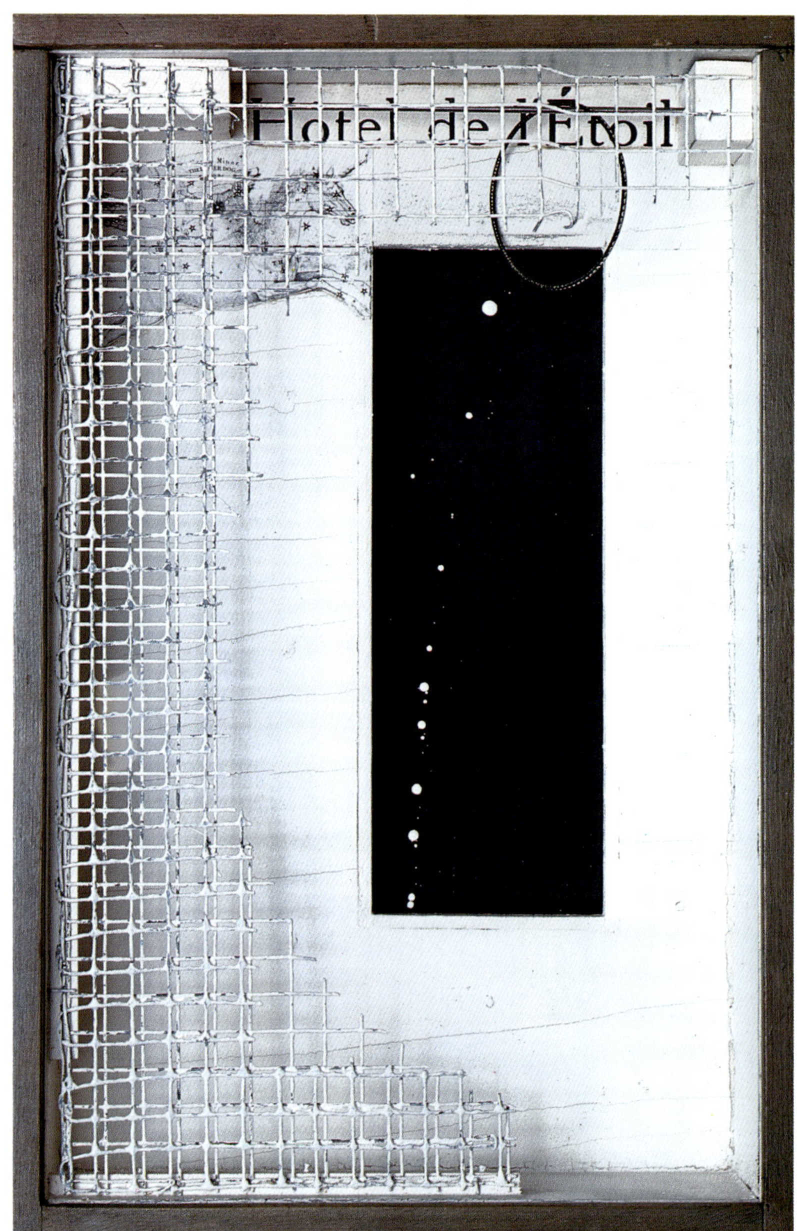

White, 1951
oil on canvas
56 x 40¼ in.

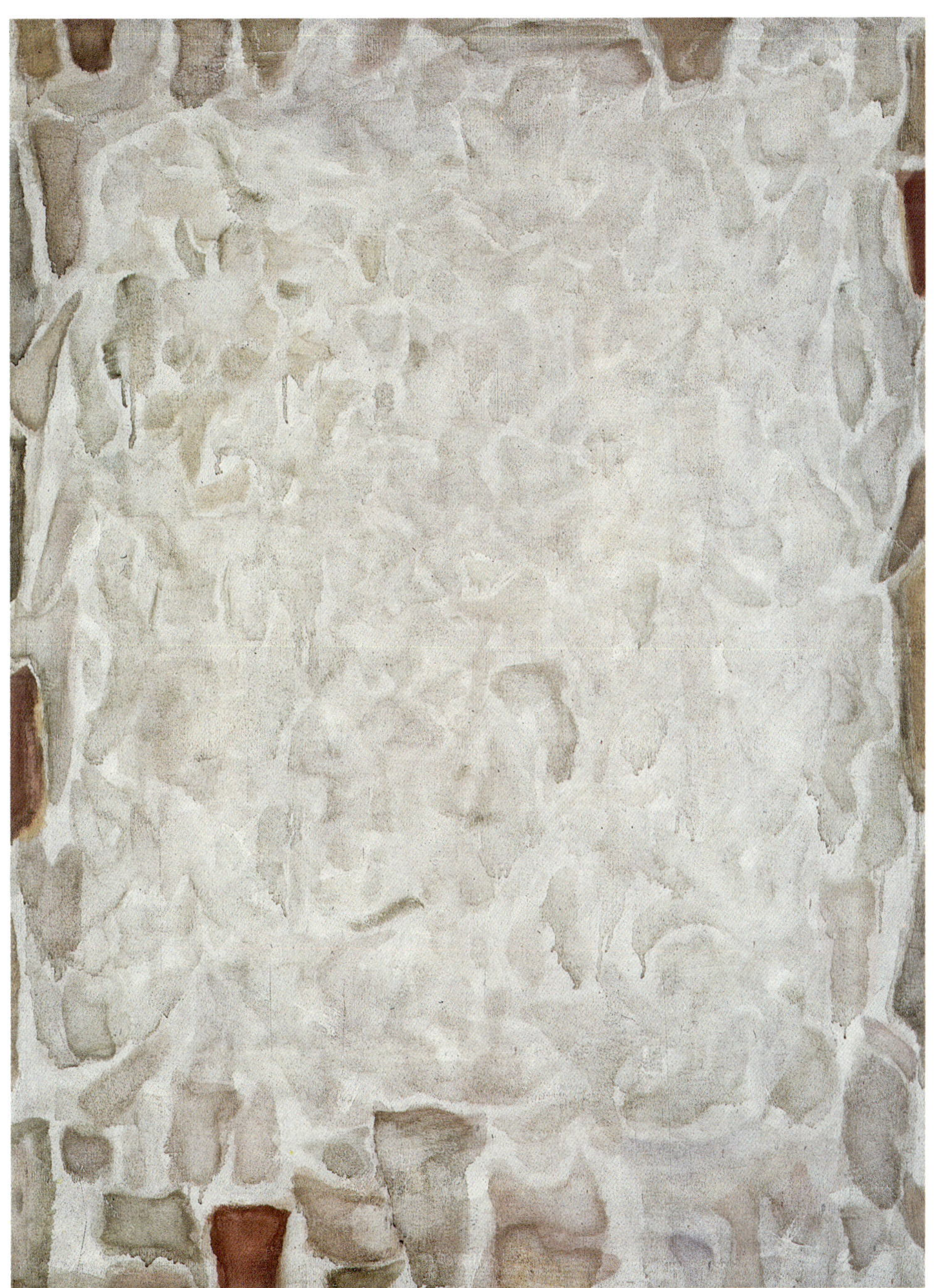

Sam Francis *(USA)*

Fruit God Fear, 1982
hand-dyed, black-and-white photographs, mounted and framed
(twenty-five parts)
118¾ x 98¾ in.

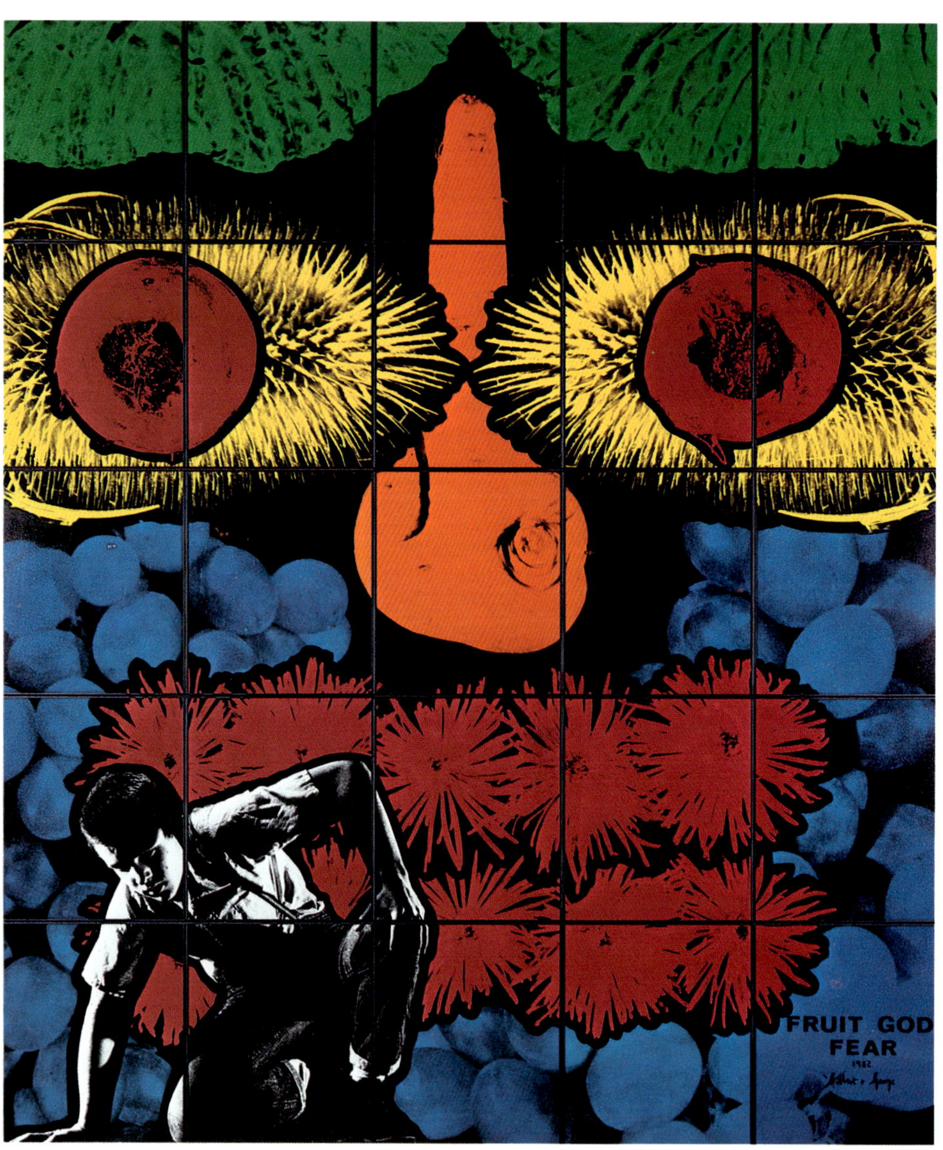

Gilbert and George (Great Britain)

Untitled, *1974*
mixed media
74 x 73 x 8 in.

Joe Goode *(USA)*

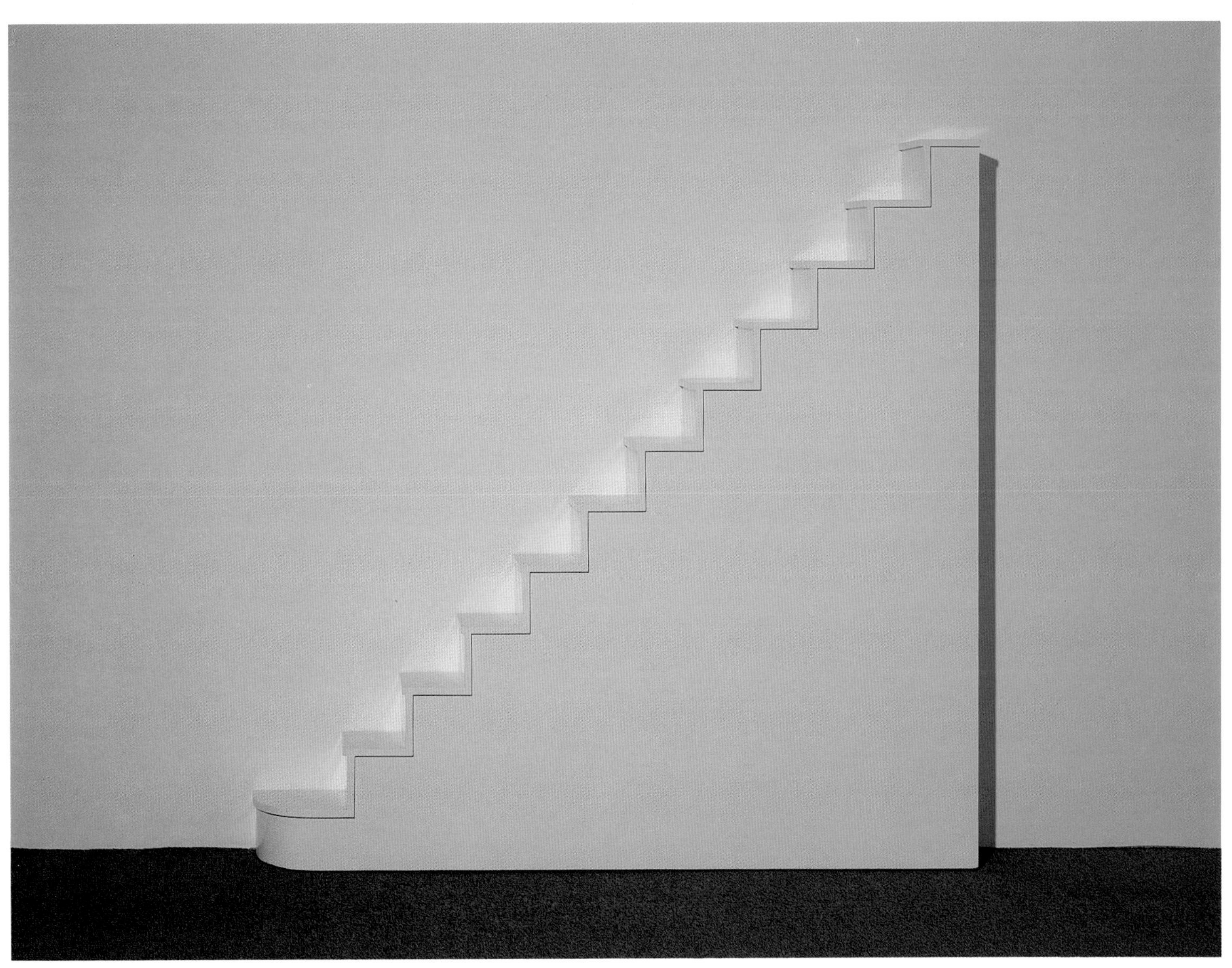

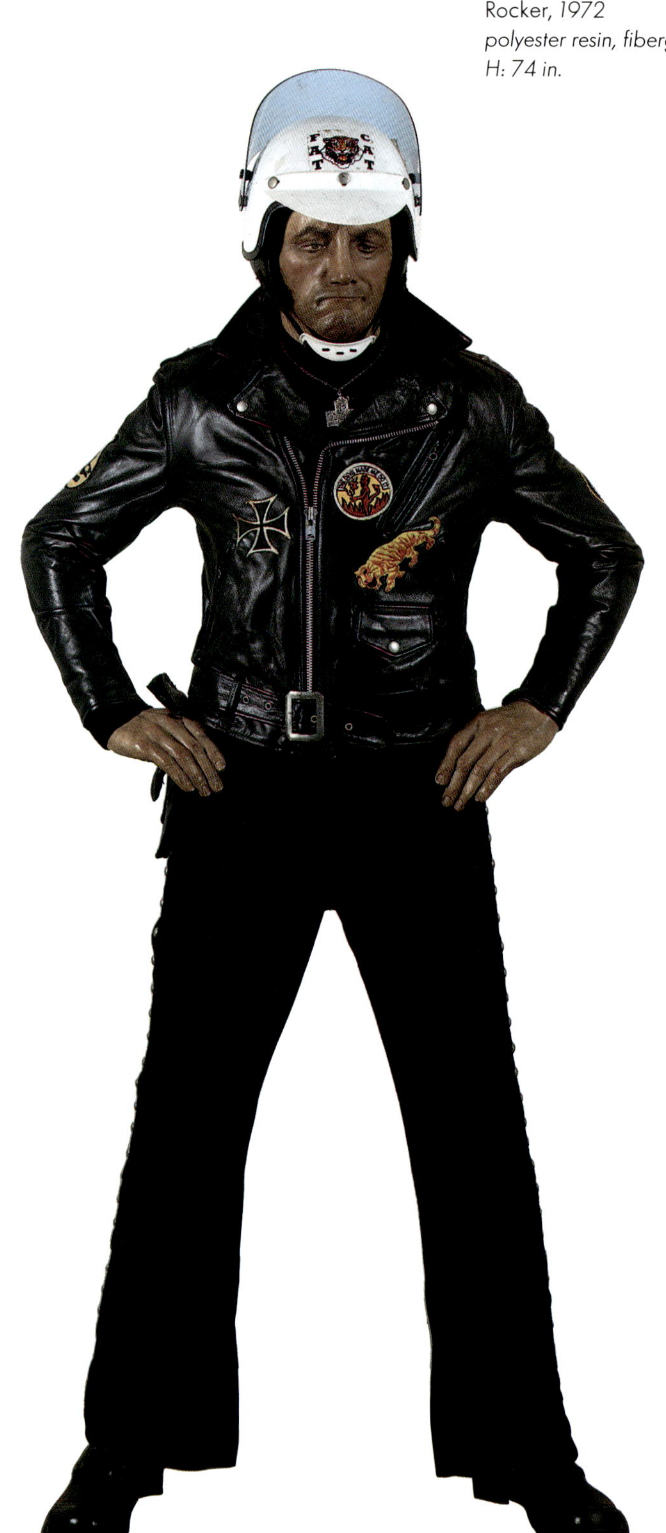

Duane Hanson *(USA)*

The Gold Coast, 1986
oil, acrylic, and sand on canvas
96 x 72½ in.

Wade Hoefer *(USA)*

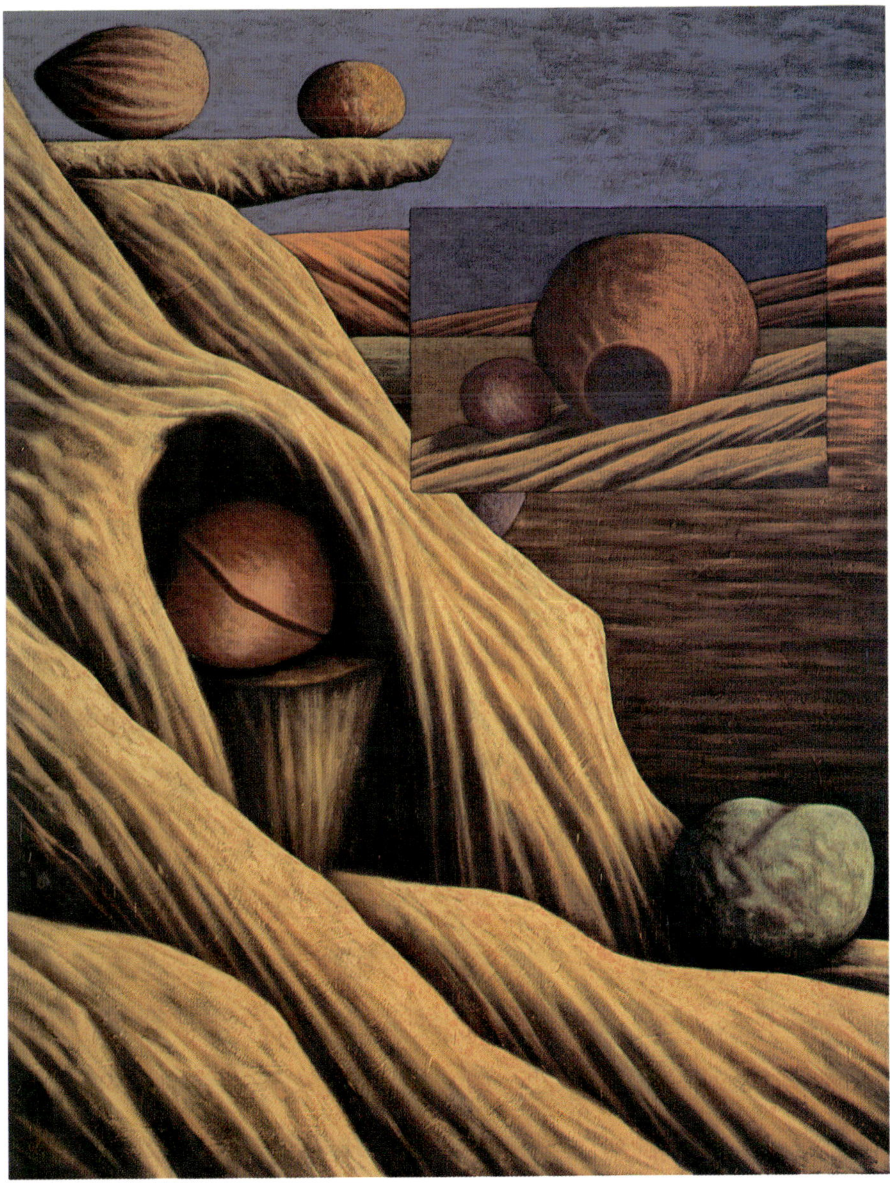

Yellow-Blue, *1965*
Vacu-form acrylic
90 x 46½ in.

Craig Kauffman *(USA)*

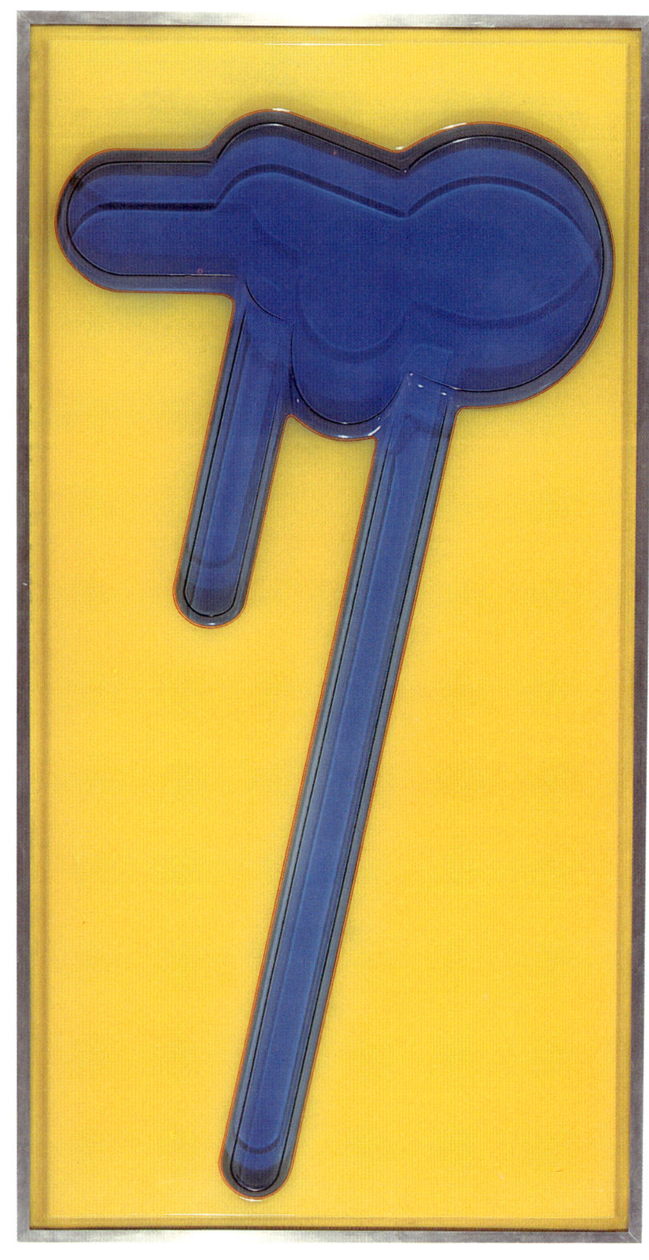

Noch ist Polen Nicht Verloren VI, *1978*
oil on burlap
83 x 106¾ in.

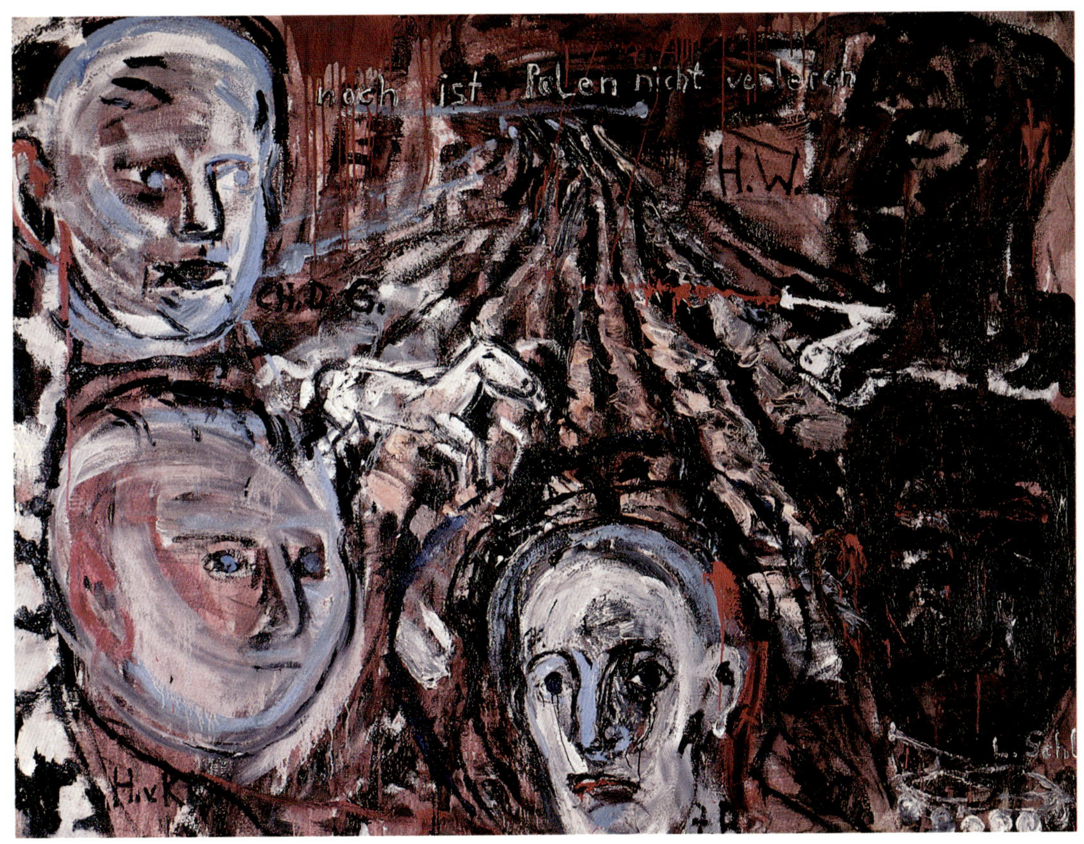

Anselm Kiefer   *(Federal Republic of Germany)*

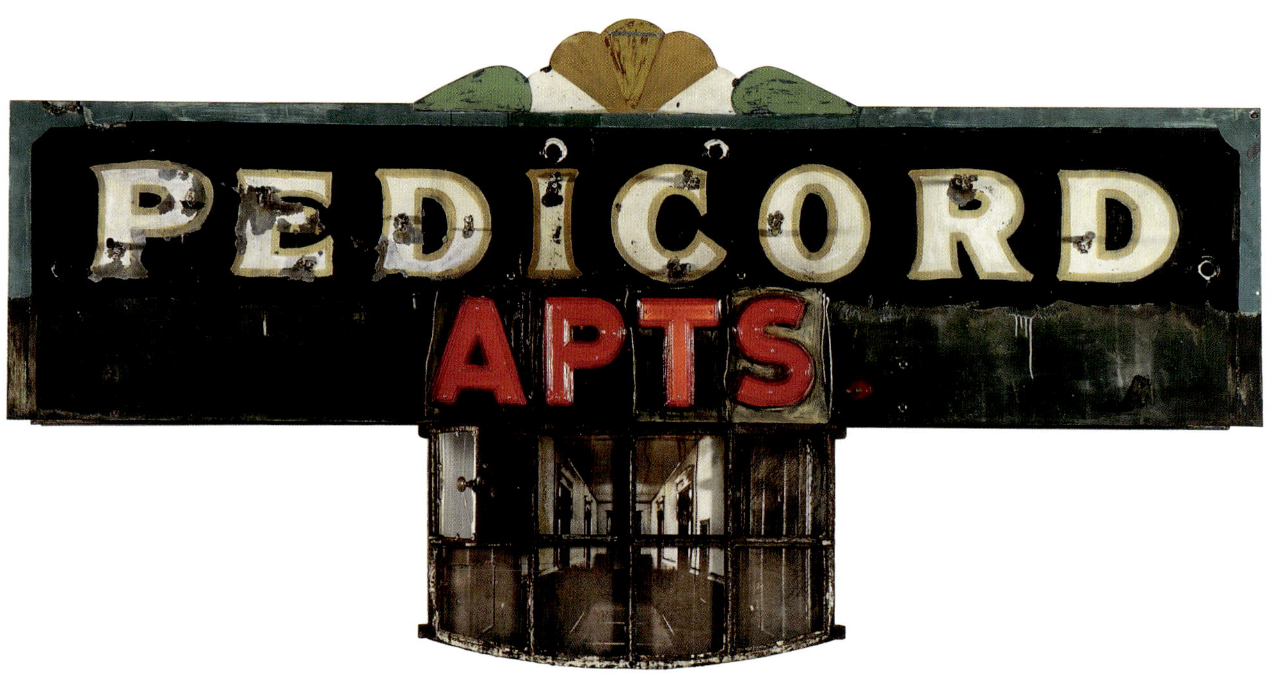

Edward and Nancy Reddin Kienholz *(USA)*

Reclining Nude, 1977
oil and magna on canvas
84 x 120 in.

Roy Lichtenstein *(USA)*

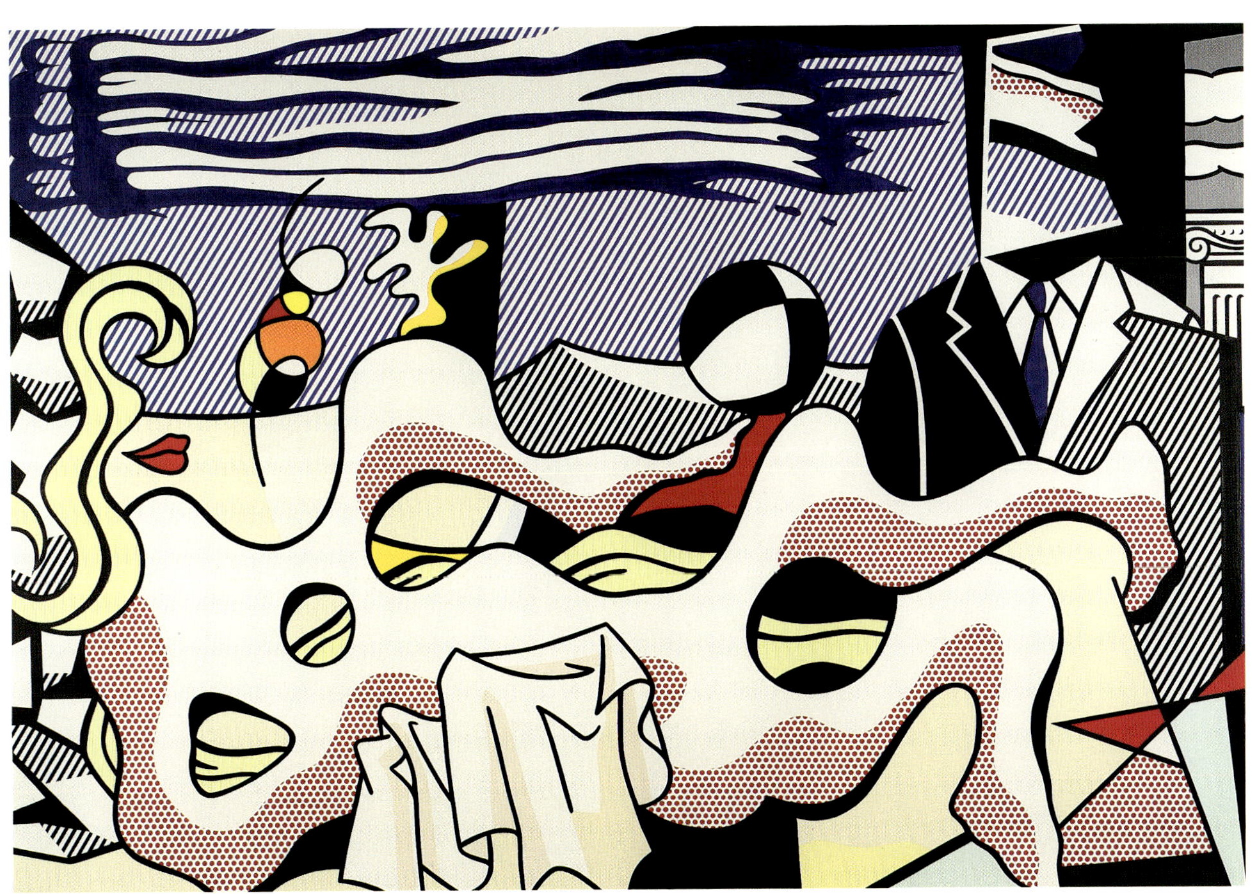

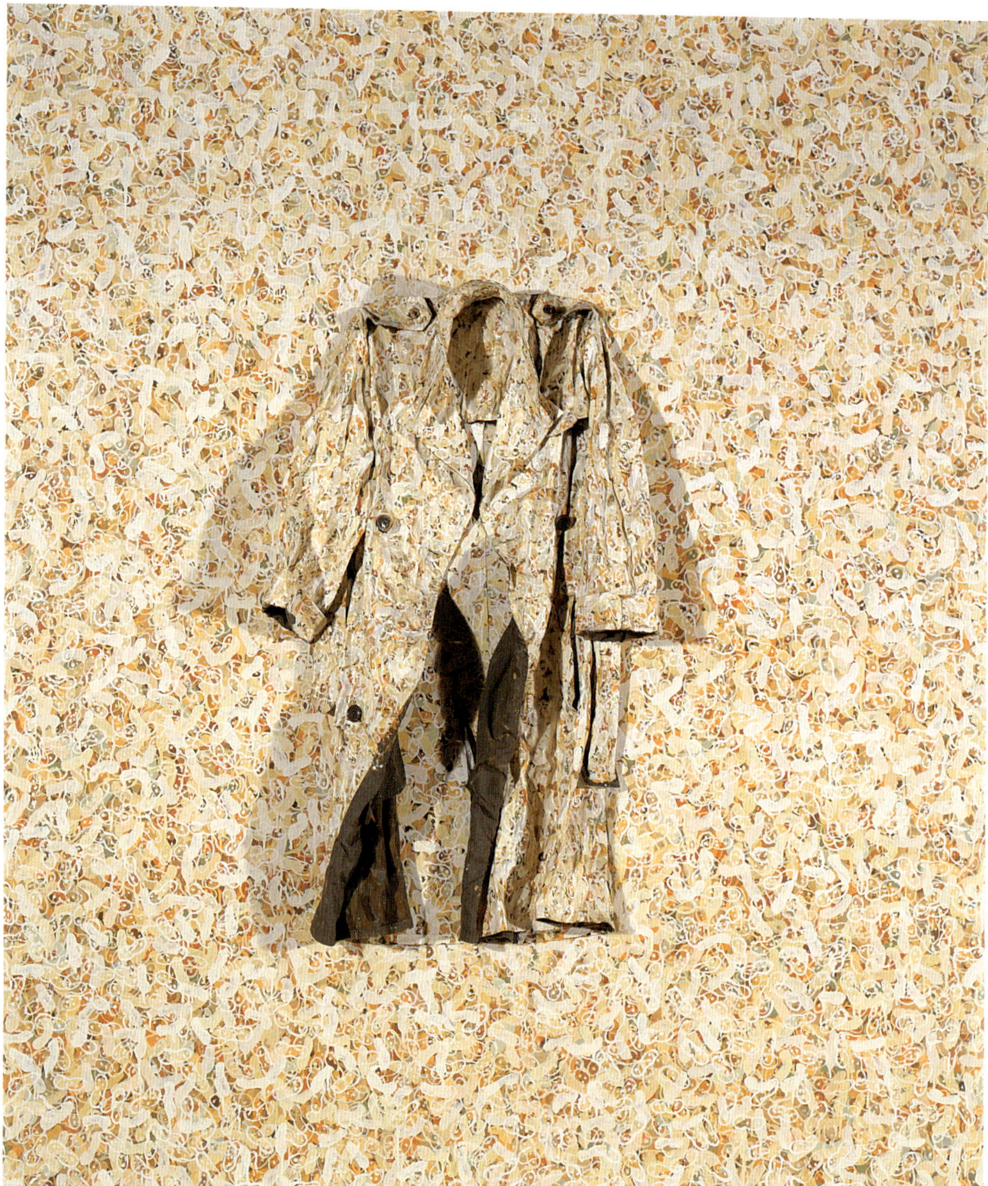

Mitsuko Miwa *(Japan)*

Untitled, 1984
oil on canvas
108 x 192 in.

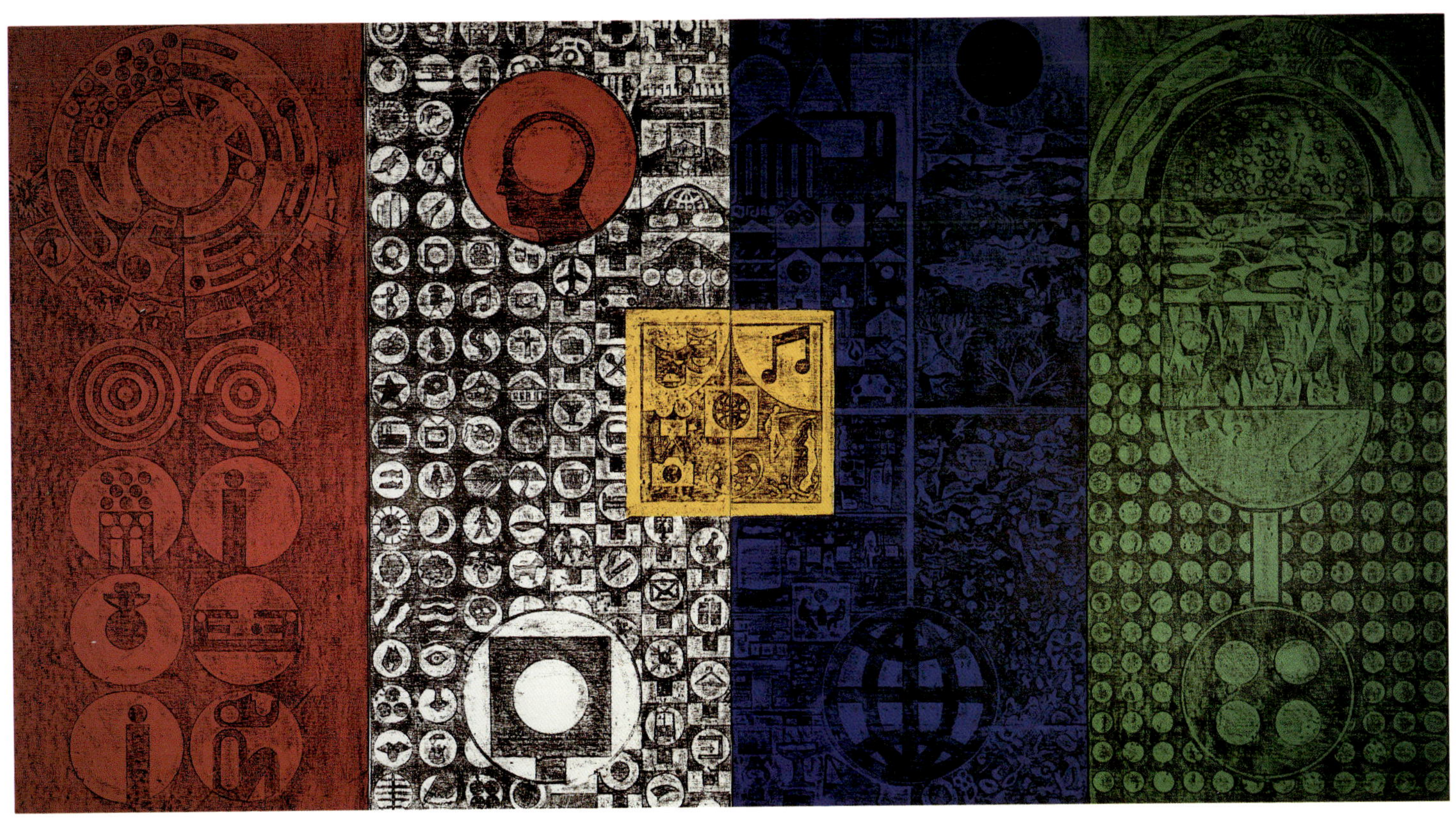

Matt Mullican *(USA)*

Barnett Newman *(USA)*

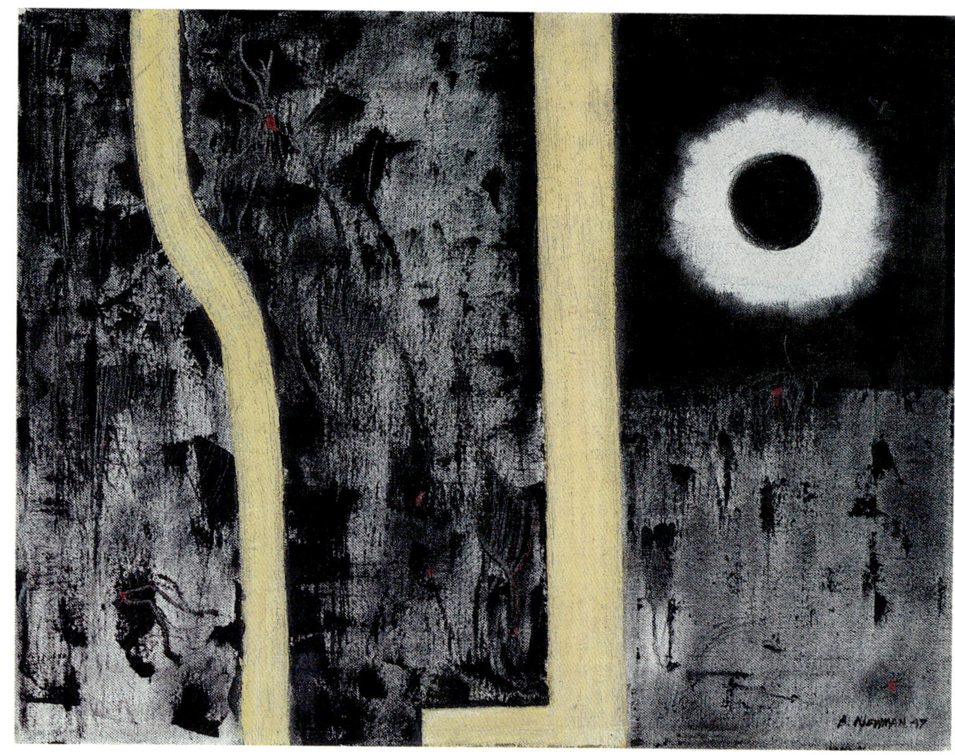

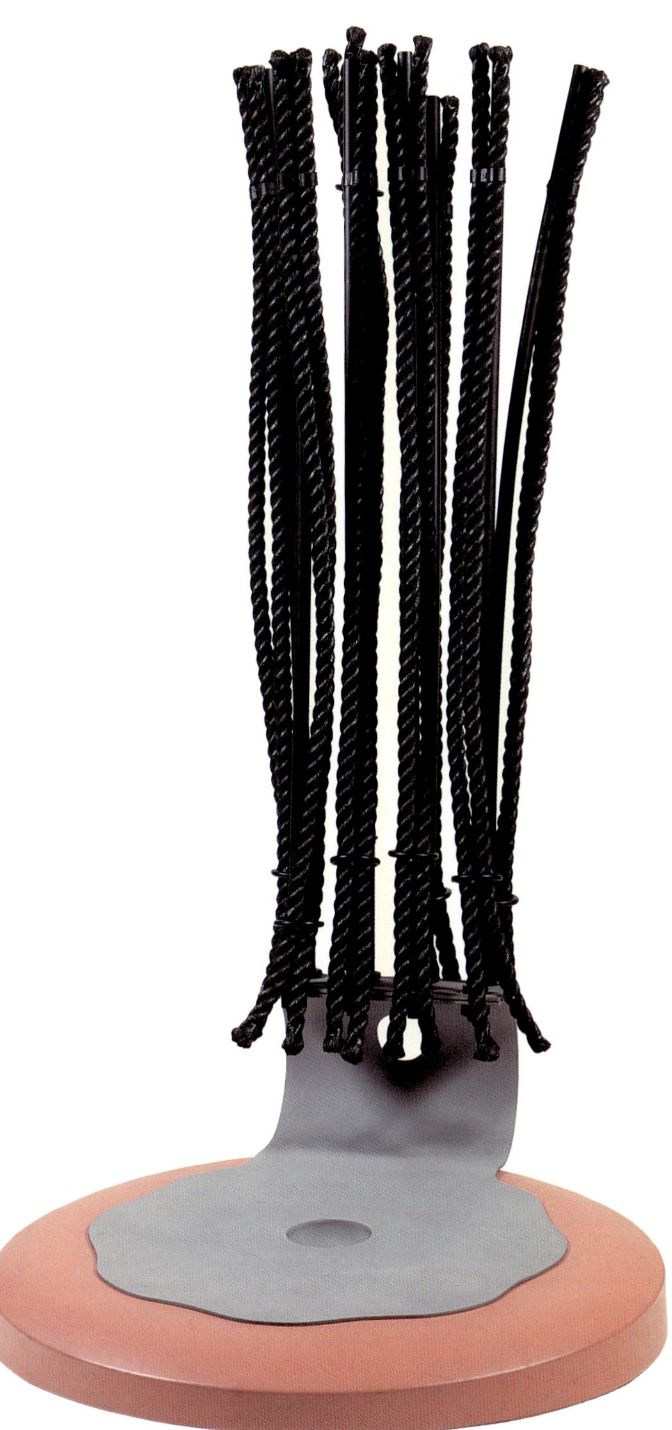

Typewriter Eraser, 1970–1975
rope, aluminum, fiberglass, and steel
84 x 48 x 48 in.

Claes Oldenburg (USA)

Please . . . , 1985
oil on canvas
59¼ x 149⅝ in.

Edward Ruscha *(USA)*

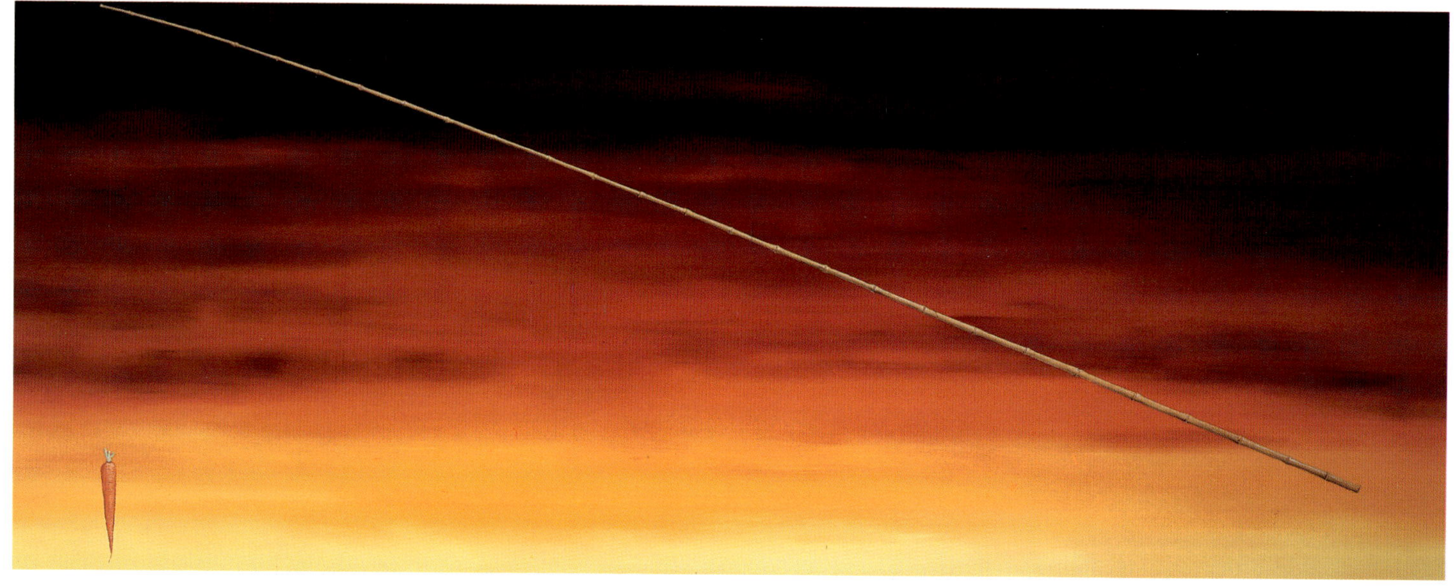

Five Guys Named Moe, 1988
wood, tin, gold leaf, paint, copper, and lead
79 x 23 x 18 in.

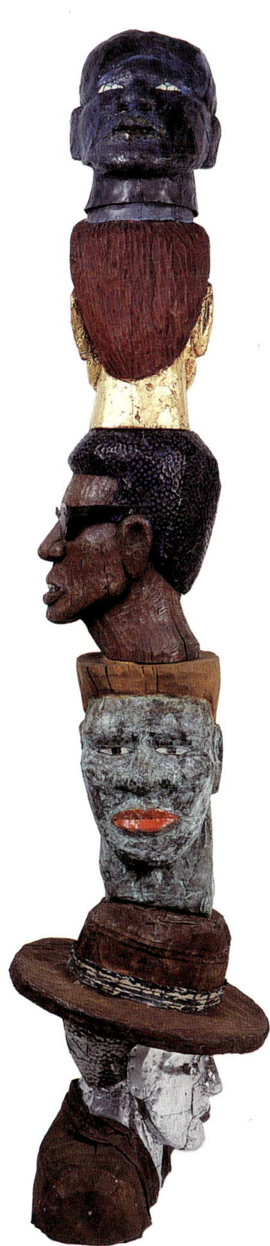

Alison Saar *(USA)*

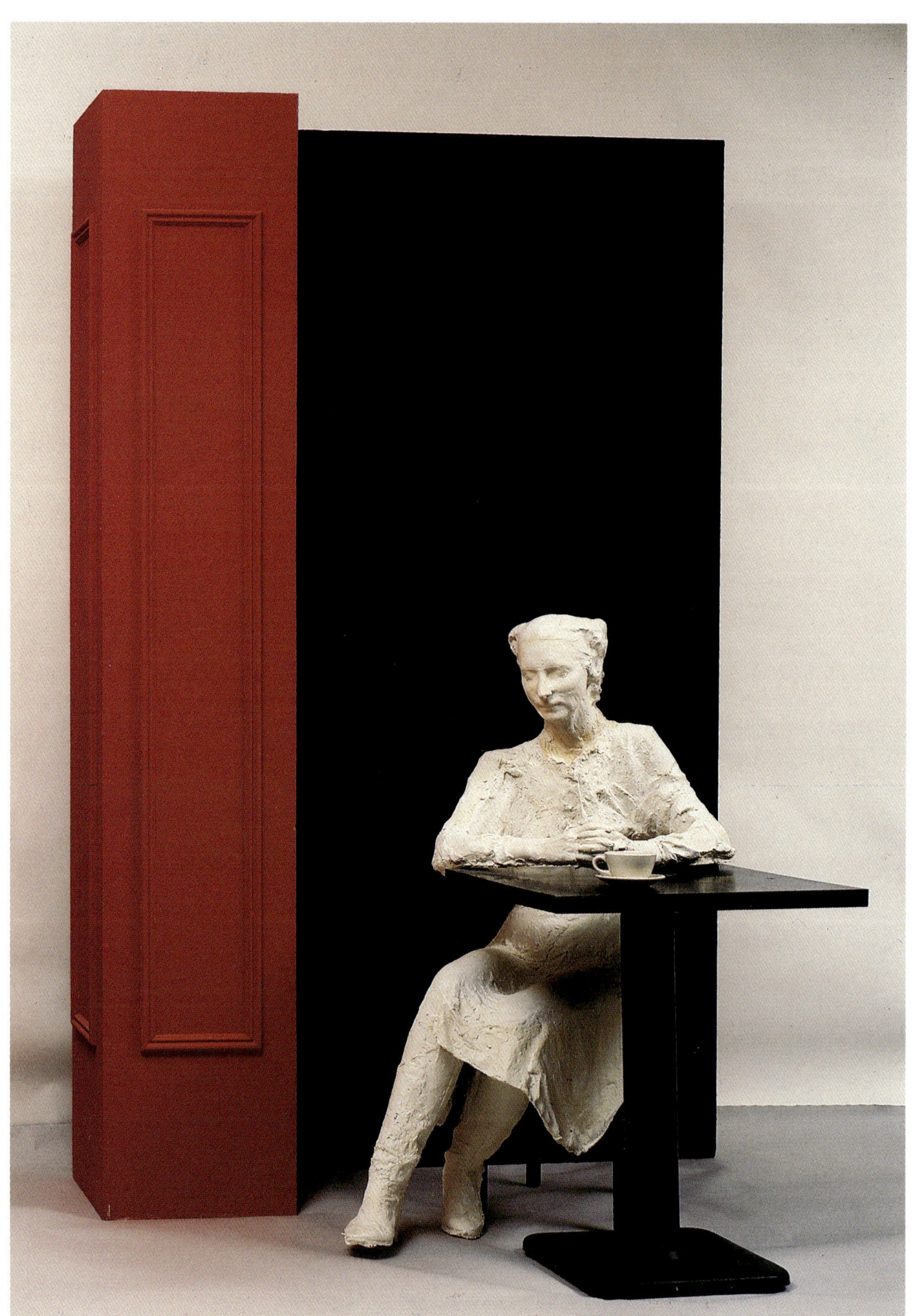

Woman in Coffee Shop, 1983
plaster, metal, plastic, wood, and glass
80 x 62 x 52 in.

George Segal (USA)

Lac Laronge (Saskatchewan series), 1967
acrylic on canvas
96 x 144 in.

Frank Stella   *(USA)*

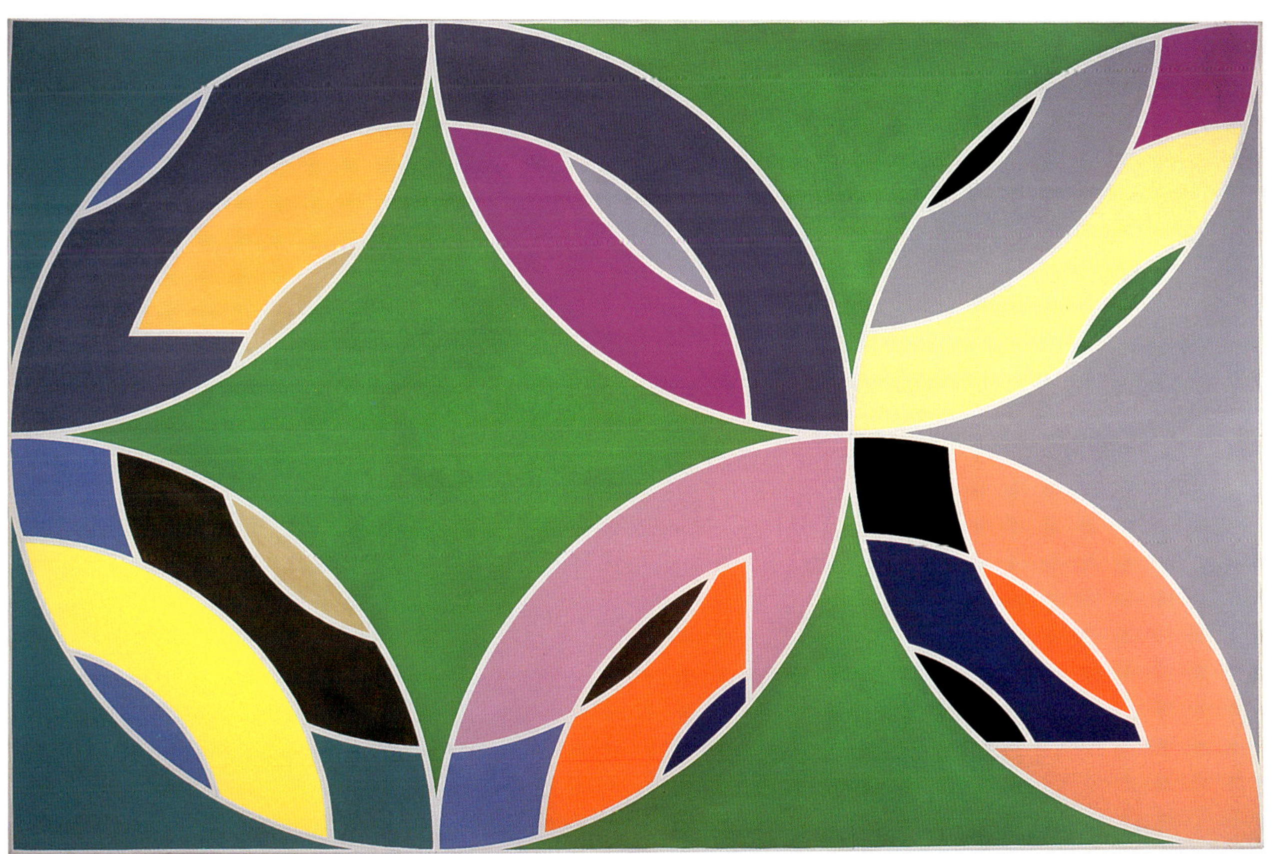

American Still Life #31, 1963
mixed media construction with television
48 x 60 x 10¾ in.

Tom Wesselmann (USA)

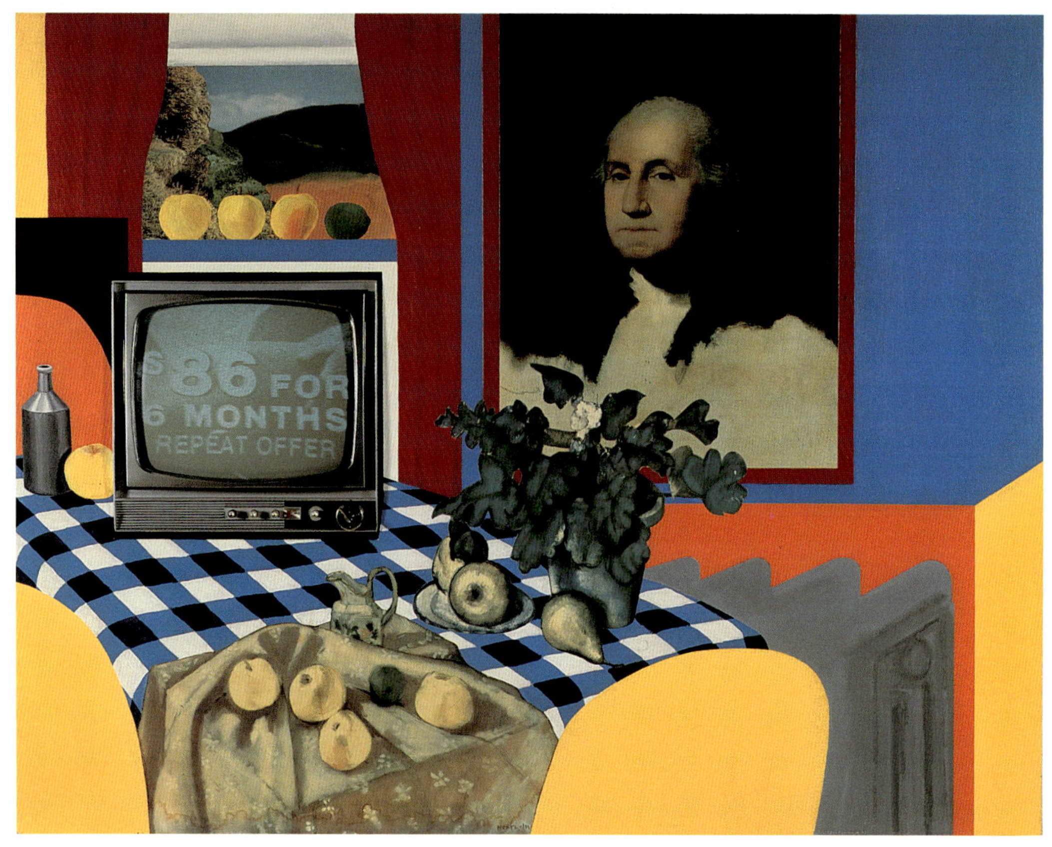
$86 FOR
6 MONTHS
REPEAT OFFER

Big Fall, 1984
oil and acrylic on canvas
72 x 132¼ in.

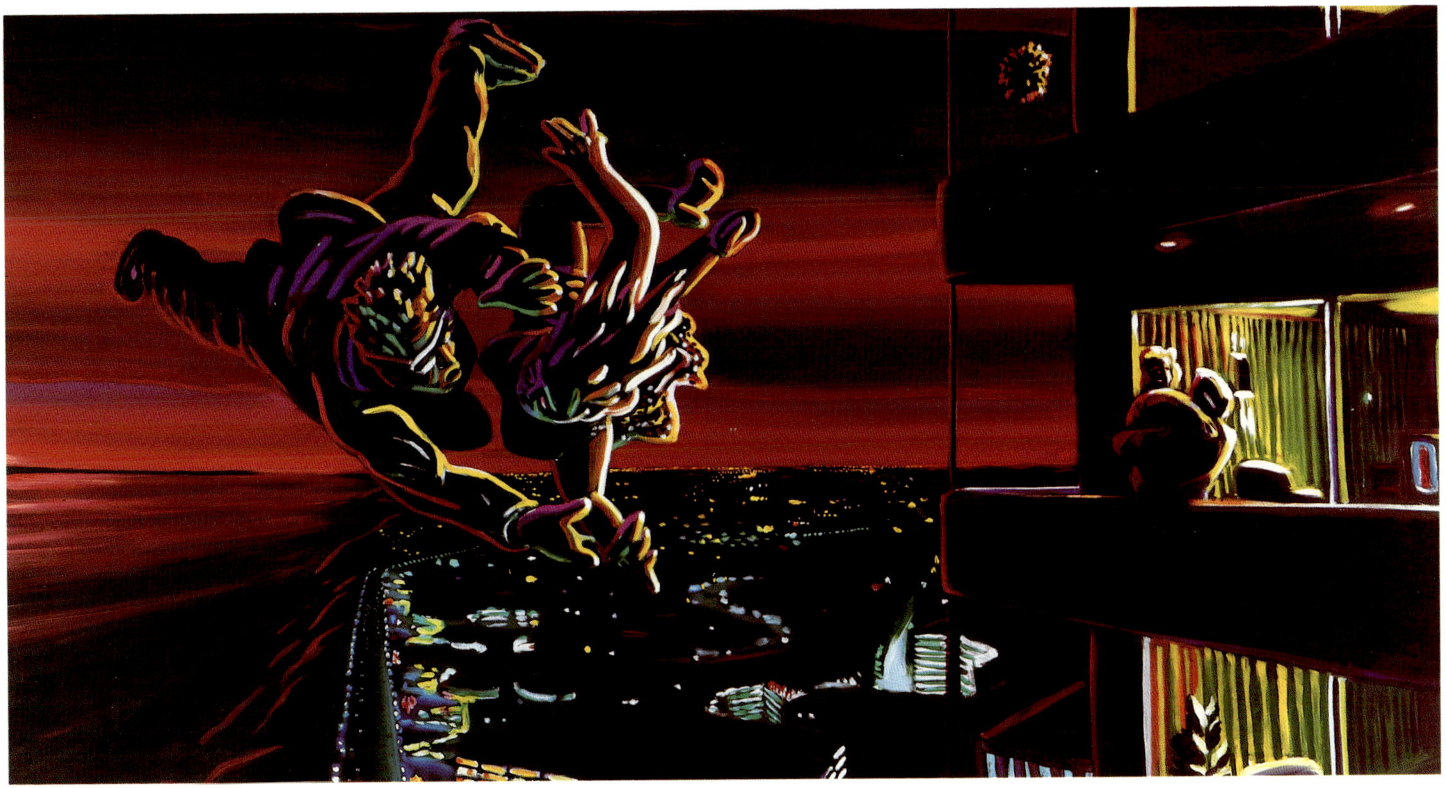

Robert Yarber *(USA)*

Shadow, 1984
mixed media with electric lights
94½ x 93½ x 12 in.

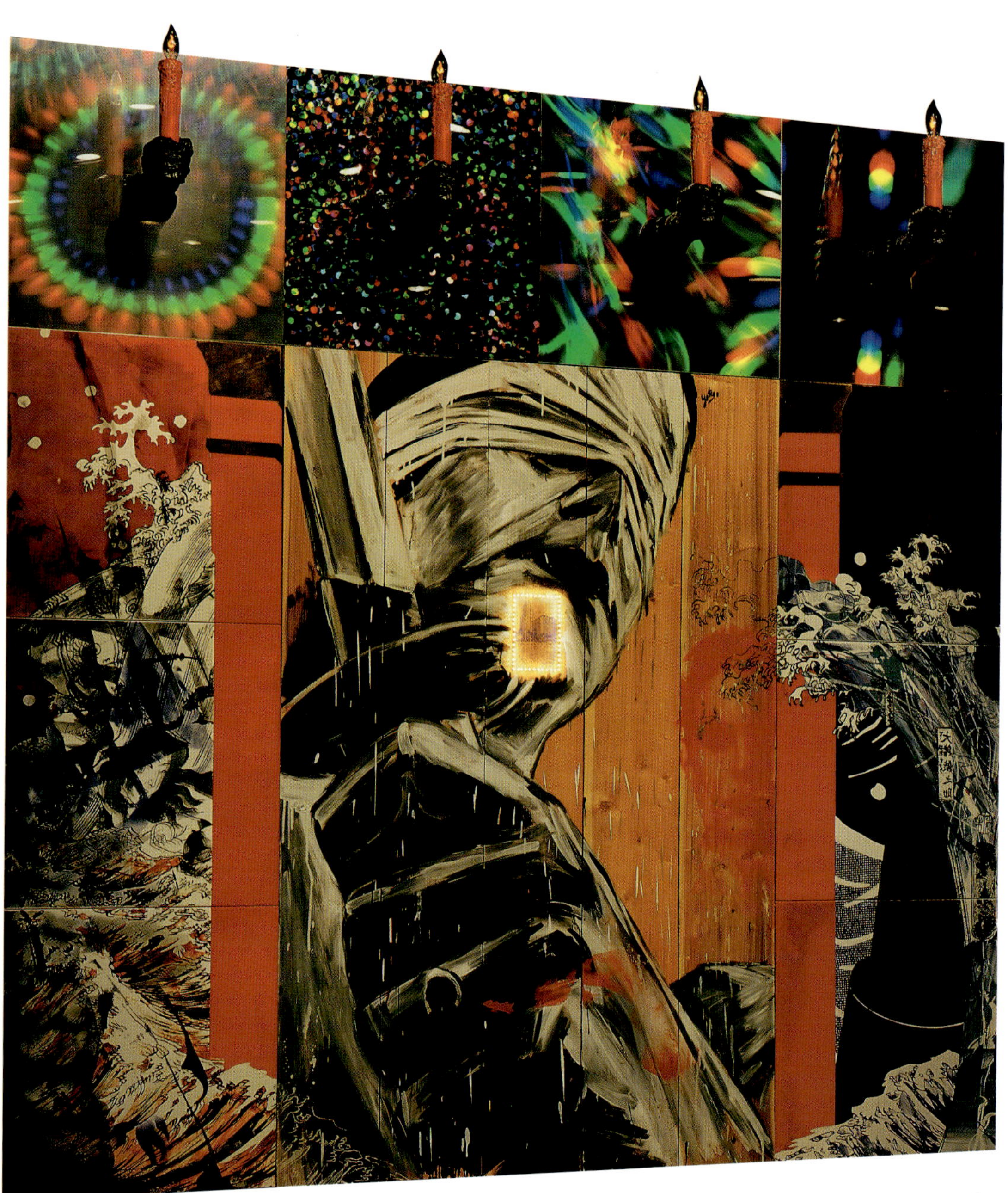

Tadanori Yokoo (Japan)

Jian-Jun Zhang *(People's Republic of China)*

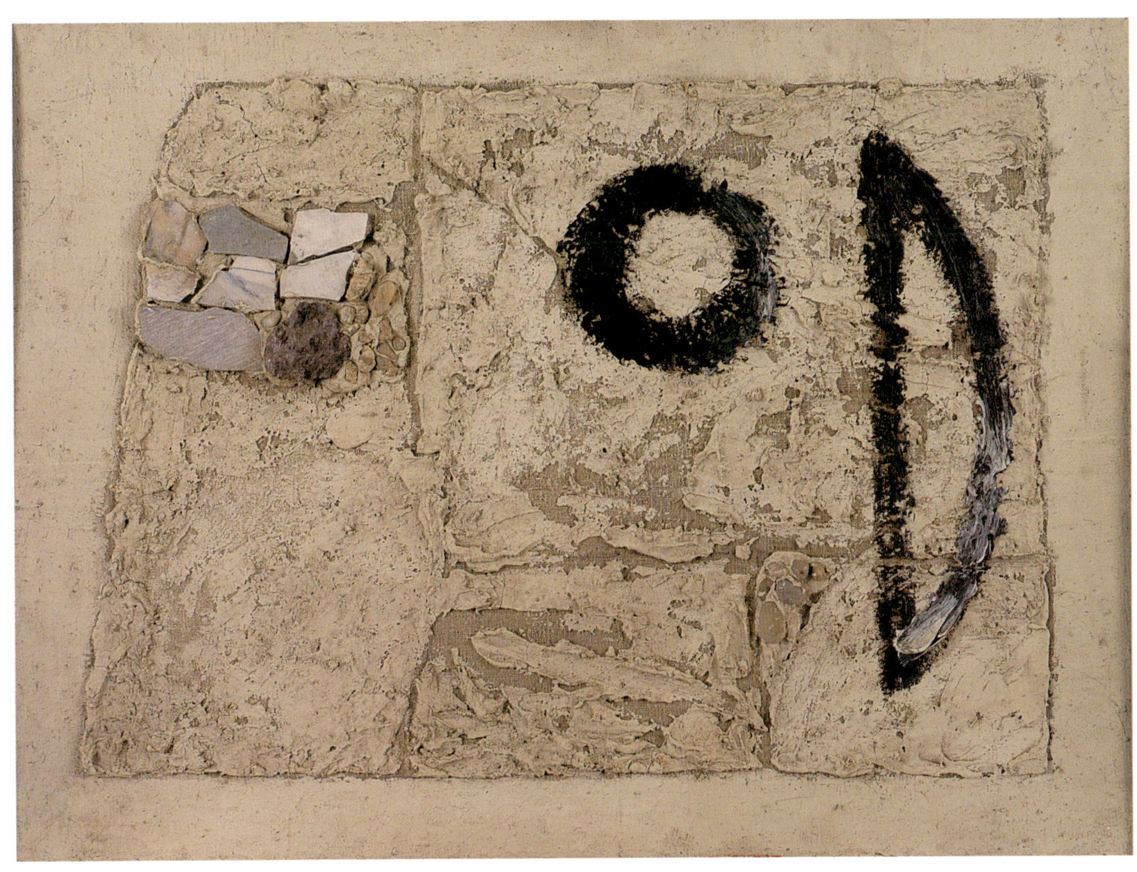